A TEXTBOOK OF PHARMACEUTICAL ANALYSIS

FOR 1ST YEAR, 1ST SEMESTER
B.PHARMACY

N.INDIRA RANI, DR. BUGGANA SIVA JYOTHI, R.SWETHA SRI

Made with ♥ on the Notion Press Platform
www.notionpress.com

Contents

Preface

It is with great pleasure that we present "A Textbook of Pharmaceutical Analysis: For 1st Year, 1st Semester B.Pharmacy". This book is designed to provide a comprehensive and in-depth understanding of the fundamental concepts and methodologies in pharmaceutical analysis, tailored specifically for first-year pharmacy students.

The field of pharmaceutical analysis is critical to the pharmaceutical industry, encompassing a wide range of techniques used to ensure the safety, efficacy, and quality of pharmaceutical products. This textbook aims to bridge the gap between theoretical principles and practical applications, providing students with a solid foundation that will be crucial for their future careers in pharmacy.

This textbook covers a broad range of topics, including volumetric analysis, electrochemical analysis, and the principles of various analytical techniques. Each chapter is meticulously structured to facilitate learning, with clear explanations, detailed procedures, and illustrative examples. We have also included numerous tables, figures, and practice problems to aid in understanding and retention of the material.

We hope this textbook serves as a valuable resource for students, helping them to develop the analytical skills necessary for their academic and professional growth. We welcome feedback and suggestions for future editions to continually improve the content and its delivery.

We extend our sincere thanks to Notion Press for their support in bringing this textbook to fruition and to our families and colleagues for their unwavering support and encouragement.

Mrs. N. Indira Rani
Dr. Buggana Siva Jyothi
Mrs. R. Swetha Sri
July 2024

A Textbook Of Pharmaceutical Analysis: For 1st Year, 1st Semester B.pharmacy

Mrs. N. Indira Rani
Assistant Professor, Department of Pharmaceutical Analysis
Sarojini Naidu Vanita Pharmacy Maha Vidyalaya
Tarnaka, Secunderabad
India
Dr. Buggana Siva Jyothi
Associate Professor, Department of Pharmaceutical Quality Assurance
Sarojini Naidu Vanita Pharmacy Maha Vidyalaya
Tarnaka, Secunderabad
India
Mrs. R. Swetha Sri
Assistant Professor, Department of Pharmaceutical Quality Assurance
Sarojini Naidu Vanita Pharmacy Maha Vidyalaya
Tarnaka, Secunderabad
India

Published by Notion Press
Notion Press, Inc.
800, West EI Camino Real #180,
California USA 94040
Notion Press Media Pvt Ltd
#7, Red Cross Road,
Egmore, Chennai, Tamil Nadu 600008
Email ID: publish@notionpress.com
Phone Number: +91 44 46315631
July 2024

ONE

INTRODUCTION TO PHARMACEUTICAL ANALYSIS

1.1 Definition and Scope of Pharmaceutical Analysis

Pharmaceutical analysis is a branch of chemistry that deals with the identification, quantification, and determination of the components in pharmaceutical products. It encompasses a wide range of methodologies and techniques to ensure the safety, efficacy, and quality of drugs. This field is crucial because it ensures that medications meet regulatory standards and are safe for consumption. The scope of pharmaceutical analysis includes a variety of techniques such as titrimetric methods, chromatographic techniques, spectroscopic methods, and electrochemical analysis. Each technique has its unique applications and advantages, which are utilized depending on the type of analysis required. For example, titrimetric methods are commonly used for determining the concentration of active ingredients, while chromatographic techniques are essential for separating and identifying complex mixtures. The primary goal of pharmaceutical analysis is to ensure that the drug products are pure, potent, and free from harmful contaminants. This requires a thorough understanding of the principles of analytical chemistry and the ability to apply these principles in a practical setting.

1.1.1 Importance in the Pharmaceutical Industry

Pharmaceutical analysis plays a vital role in the pharmaceutical industry. It is integral to the development, production, and quality assurance of pharmaceutical products. **Ensuring drug safety and efficacy** is one of the primary responsibilities of pharmaceutical analysis. For instance, during the drug development phase, rigorous analytical testing is conducted to determine the chemical composition and stability of new drug entities. This process includes various stages such as pre-formulation, formulation development, and stability testing. Analytical methods are used to identify the presence of impurities, which can affect the safety and efficacy of the drug. For example, impurities in active pharmaceutical ingredients (APIs) can lead to adverse effects in patients or reduce the effectiveness of the drug.

Moreover, pharmaceutical analysis is essential for **regulatory compliance**. The pharmaceutical industry is highly regulated, with stringent guidelines set by organizations such as the Food and Drug Administration (FDA), European Medicines Agency (EMA), and the Indian Pharmacopoeia Commission (IPC). These guidelines require comprehensive analytical testing to ensure that products meet specified standards. Failure to comply with these regulations can result in severe consequences, including product recalls, legal actions, and loss of consumer trust. In addition, analytical methods are used in **patent protection** and **intellectual property**. By characterizing the molecular structure and composition of new drugs, pharmaceutical companies can secure patents and protect their innovations from competitors.

Another critical aspect of pharmaceutical analysis is its role in **research and development (R&D)**. Analytical techniques are used to investigate the pharmacokinetics and pharmacodynamics of drugs, which involves studying how the drug is absorbed, distributed, metabolized, and excreted in the body. This information is crucial for optimizing drug formulations and determining appropriate dosage regimens. For example, high-performance liquid chromatography (HPLC) is frequently used in bioanalytical studies to measure drug concentrations in biological samples.

Furthermore, pharmaceutical analysis contributes to **cost efficiency** in manufacturing. By ensuring that raw materials and finished products meet quality standards, pharmaceutical companies can minimize waste and reduce production costs. Analytical testing helps identify and eliminate inefficiencies in the manufacturing process, leading to higher yields and better resource utilization. In essence, pharmaceutical analysis is indispensable for maintaining the integrity of the pharmaceutical industry. It ensures that drugs are safe, effective, and of high quality, thereby protecting public health and enhancing the credibility of pharmaceutical companies.

1.1.2 Role in Quality Control and Assurance

Quality control (QC) and quality assurance (QA) are critical components of the pharmaceutical industry, and pharmaceutical analysis is at the heart of these processes. **Quality control** involves the routine testing of pharmaceutical products to ensure they meet predefined quality standards. This includes testing raw materials, in-process materials, and finished products. Analytical methods are used to verify that each batch of a drug product is consistent in terms of potency, purity, and overall quality. For example, a common QC test might involve using **titration** to determine the concentration of an active ingredient in a drug formulation. This ensures that each dose contains the correct amount of medication, which is essential for efficacy and patient safety.

In contrast, **quality assurance** is a broader concept that encompasses all aspects of ensuring the quality of pharmaceutical products, from development through production to distribution. QA includes establishing and maintaining a quality management system (QMS) that complies with regulatory requirements and industry standards. **Pharmaceutical analysis** plays a pivotal role in QA by providing the data needed to make informed decisions about product quality. For instance, **stability testing** is a critical aspect of QA. Analytical methods are used to evaluate how a drug product behaves under various environmental conditions, such as temperature, humidity, and light. Stability testing helps determine the shelf life of a product and ensures that it remains effective and safe throughout its intended storage period.

Another important aspect of QA is **validation and verification**. Analytical methods must be validated to ensure they are reliable, accurate, and reproducible. This involves rigorous testing and documentation to confirm that the methods perform as expected. For example, the validation of an HPLC method might include tests for specificity, linearity, accuracy, precision, and robustness. Once validated, these methods are used to verify that all aspects of the manufacturing process consistently produce a product that meets quality standards. **In-process control (IPC)** is another QA activity that relies heavily on pharmaceutical analysis. IPC involves monitoring and controlling various parameters during the manufacturing process to ensure that the final product meets quality specifications. Analytical techniques are used to measure critical attributes such as particle size, moisture content, and dissolution rate. For instance, near-infrared (NIR) spectroscopy can be used for real-time monitoring of tablet composition during production.

Documentation and record-keeping are also essential components of QA. All analytical data must be accurately recorded and maintained to provide a complete history of each batch of product. This documentation is crucial for traceability, regulatory compliance, and in case of any quality issues or recalls. **Audits and inspections** by regulatory agencies also rely on pharmaceutical analysis. During these audits, inspectors review analytical data and procedures to ensure that the company is adhering to good manufacturing practices (GMP) and other regulatory requirements. Having robust analytical methods and thorough documentation can help demonstrate compliance and avoid regulatory actions.

1.2 Techniques of Analysis

1.2.1 Overview of Analytical Techniques

Analytical techniques are the methods used to determine the composition and quality of pharmaceutical substances. These techniques are critical for ensuring the safety, efficacy, and quality of drugs. They encompass a wide range of methods, each with unique applications and advantages.

Chromatographic Techniques: These methods are used for separating mixtures into their individual components. Common types include **high-performance liquid chromatography (HPLC)**, **gas chromatography (GC)**, and **thin-layer chromatography (TLC)**. HPLC is widely used for the quantification of drugs in various formulations due to its high resolution and sensitivity. For example, HPLC can separate and quantify the active ingredients in a complex drug formulation, ensuring the correct dosage and identifying impurities.

Spectroscopic Techniques: These methods involve the interaction of light with matter to identify and quantify substances. **Ultraviolet-visible (UV-Vis) spectroscopy**, **infrared (IR) spectroscopy**, and **nuclear magnetic resonance (NMR) spectroscopy** are commonly used in pharmaceutical analysis. UV-Vis spectroscopy, for example, is often used to determine the concentration of a drug in solution by measuring the absorbance of light at specific wavelengths.

Electrochemical Techniques: These methods are based on the measurement of electrical properties such as voltage, current, or resistance. Techniques like **potentiometry**, **voltammetry**, and **conductometry** are used for analyzing ionic substances. Potentiometry, which involves measuring the voltage of an electrochemical cell, is commonly used for determining the pH of solutions and the concentration of ions.

Titrimetric Methods: These are classical analytical methods involving the measurement of the volume of a solution required to react with a known quantity of analyte. **Acid-base titration**, **redox titration**, **complexometric titration**, and **precipitation titration** are widely used. For example, acid-base titration is used to determine the concentration of acidic or basic substances by neutralizing them with a base or acid of known concentration.

Mass Spectrometry (MS): This technique is used for identifying the molecular structure and composition of substances by measuring the mass-to-charge ratio of ions. MS is highly sensitive and can detect very low concentrations of substances, making it invaluable for identifying impurities and degradation products in pharmaceuticals.

Each of these analytical techniques has specific applications and is chosen based on the nature of the analyte and the required sensitivity and specificity. The combination of these techniques provides a comprehensive approach to pharmaceutical analysis, ensuring that drugs are safe, effective, and of high quality.

1.2.2 Qualitative and Quantitative Analysis

Qualitative Analysis: This type of analysis is concerned with identifying the components of a substance. It provides information about the chemical composition and structure of the analyte. Techniques such as **mass spectrometry (MS)**, **infrared (IR) spectroscopy**, and **nuclear magnetic resonance (NMR) spectroscopy** are commonly used for qualitative analysis. For instance, MS can be used to determine the molecular weight and structural information of a compound, while IR spectroscopy can identify functional groups based on the absorption of infrared light at specific wavelengths. Qualitative analysis is crucial for ensuring that the correct compounds are present in a pharmaceutical product and for identifying any impurities or degradation products.

Quantitative Analysis: This type of analysis measures the amount or concentration of a substance in a sample. Techniques like **high-performance liquid chromatography (HPLC)**, **gas chromatography (GC)**, and **UV-visible (UV-Vis) spectroscopy** are commonly used for quantitative analysis. For example, HPLC can accurately measure the concentration of active pharmaceutical ingredients (APIs) in a formulation by separating the components and quantifying them based on their retention times and peak areas. UV-Vis spectroscopy, on the other hand, measures the absorbance of light by a sample at specific wavelengths, allowing for the determination of the concentration of analytes based on their absorbance properties.

Combination of Qualitative and Quantitative Analysis: In many cases, a combination of qualitative and quantitative analysis is used to provide a complete understanding of a pharmaceutical product. For instance, a drug formulation might first be analyzed qualitatively using NMR spectroscopy to confirm the presence of the correct active ingredients and then quantitatively using HPLC to ensure that these ingredients are present in the correct concentrations. This combined approach ensures both the identity and the quantity of the components, which is essential for the efficacy and safety of the drug.

1.3 Methods of Expressing Concentration

1.3.1 Molarity

Molarity (M) is defined as the number of moles of solute dissolved in one liter of solution. It is a widely used unit of concentration in chemistry and pharmaceuticals due to its straightforward relationship with the amount of substance and the volume of solution. Molarity is expressed in moles per liter (mol/L). For example, a 1 M solution of sodium chloride (NaCl) contains one mole of NaCl in one liter of solution.

Formula for Molarity:

M = (moles of solute) / (liters of solution)

To prepare a molar solution, you need to dissolve the appropriate amount of solute in a volume of solvent to reach the desired final volume. For instance, to prepare 1 liter of a 1 M NaCl solution, you would dissolve 58.44 grams (the molar mass of NaCl) in water and then dilute it to a final volume of 1 liter.

Molarity is particularly useful in stoichiometric calculations for reactions occurring in solution, as it allows for easy conversion between volume and moles of reactants or products.

1.3.2 Normality

Normality (N) is another unit of concentration that measures the gram equivalent weight of solute per liter of solution. It is commonly used in titration calculations, where the reactive capacity of the solute is important. Normality takes into account the equivalent factor, which is the number of moles of reactive units in a molecule.

Formula for Normality:

N = (gram equivalents of solute) / (liters of solution)

To find the normality, you first need to determine the equivalent weight of the solute, which depends on the type of reaction it undergoes. For instance, in acid-base reactions, the equivalent weight is the molar mass divided by the number of protons (H^+) the acid can donate or the base can accept. For HCl, the equivalent weight is equal to its molar mass (36.46 g/mol), as it donates one proton.

Normality is particularly useful for acid-base titrations, redox reactions, and precipitation reactions, where the equivalent factor simplifies calculations and provides a direct measure of reactive capacity.

1.3.3 Other Concentration Units

Apart from molarity and normality, several other units of concentration are used depending on the context and precision required:

Molality (m): Defined as the number of moles of solute per kilogram of solvent. It is useful in thermodynamic calculations where temperature changes, as it does not depend on volume, which can change with temperature.

Formula for Molality:

m = (moles of solute) / (kilograms of solvent)

Formality (F): Similar to molarity, but it refers to the formula units of solute per liter of solution, often used for ionic compounds that dissociate in solution.

Mole Fraction (χ): The ratio of the number of moles of one component to the total number of moles of all components in the mixture. It is a dimensionless quantity and is useful in expressing the concentration in gases and solutions.

Formula for Mole Fraction:

χ = (moles of component) / (total moles of all components)

Volume Percent (v/v%): The volume of solute divided by the total volume of the solution, multiplied by 100. Commonly used in solutions of liquids.

Formula for Volume Percent (v/v%):

Volume percent = (volume of solute / total volume of solution) × 100

1.3.4 Percent Composition

Percent composition expresses the concentration of a component in a mixture or solution as a percentage of the total. It can be expressed in different ways depending on the nature of the mixture:

Weight Percent (w/w%): The mass of solute divided by the total mass of the solution, multiplied by 100. It is commonly used in solid and liquid mixtures.

Formula for Weight Percent (w/w%):

Weight percent = (mass of solute / total mass of solution) × 100

Weight/Volume Percent (w/v%): The mass of solute divided by the volume of solution, multiplied by 100. This is frequently used in pharmaceutical formulations.

Formula for Weight/Volume Percent (w/v%):

Weight/volume percent = (mass of solute (g) / volume of solution (mL)) × 100

1.3.5 Parts per Million (PPM) and Parts per Billion (PPB)

Parts per million (PPM) and **parts per billion (PPB)** are units used to express very low concentrations of substances. They are particularly useful in environmental analysis, toxicology, and quality control in pharmaceuticals where trace amounts of impurities or contaminants need to be measured.

PPM: Represents one part of solute per million parts of solution (or mixture). It is equivalent to milligrams of solute per liter of solution (mg/L) for dilute aqueous solutions.

Formula for PPM:

PPM = (mass of solute / total mass of solution) × 10^6

PPB: Represents one part of solute per billion parts of solution. It is equivalent to micrograms of solute per liter of solution (μg/L) for dilute aqueous solutions.

Formula for PPB:

PPB = (mass of solute / total mass of solution) × 10^9

These units allow for the precise measurement and expression of very low concentrations, essential for ensuring the safety and efficacy of pharmaceutical products. For example, the allowable limit of heavy metals in a drug might be specified in PPM to ensure patient safety.

1.4 Primary and Secondary Standards

1.4.1 Definition and Examples

Primary Standards are highly pure substances that serve as reference materials in quantitative analysis. They have specific characteristics that make them ideal for use in calibration and standardization processes. These characteristics include high purity, stability under storage conditions, non-hygroscopic nature (they do not absorb moisture from the air), and a high molecular weight to minimize weighing errors. Because of their high degree of purity, primary standards provide a definitive measure of the amount of substance present, allowing for precise and accurate standardization of solutions.

Examples of Primary Standards:

- **Potassium Hydrogen Phthalate (KHP)**: Often used in the standardization of basic solutions due to its high purity and stability.
- **Sodium Carbonate (Na$_2$CO$_3$)**: Commonly used in acid-base titrations to standardize acidic solutions.
- **Silver Nitrate (AgNO$_3$)**: Used in precipitation titrations, especially for the standardization of chloride solutions.
- **Benzoic Acid (C$_6$H$_5$COOH)**: Utilized in calorimetry and as a primary standard for standardizing basic solutions.

Secondary Standards are substances whose purity and composition have been established by comparison with primary standards. These standards are used for routine analysis and calibration of analytical instruments. Secondary standards are often used when primary standards are not available or practical for certain applications. They are typically standardized against primary standards to ensure their accuracy and reliability in quantitative analysis.

Examples of Secondary Standards:

- **Hydrochloric Acid (HCl)**: Often used as a secondary standard in titrations after being standardized against a primary standard like sodium carbonate.
- **Sodium Hydroxide (NaOH)**: Commonly used in titrations as a secondary standard after standardization with primary standards such as potassium hydrogen phthalate.
- **EDTA (Ethylenediaminetetraacetic Acid)**: Used in complexometric titrations and standardized against primary standards like calcium carbonate.

1.4.2 Importance and Applications

Importance of Primary and Secondary Standards:

1. **Accuracy and Precision**: Primary standards provide a reliable reference point, ensuring that the concentrations of solutions used in quantitative analysis are accurate and precise. This accuracy is crucial for achieving consistent and reproducible results in analytical procedures.

2. **Validation and Calibration**: Primary and secondary standards are essential for the calibration of analytical instruments and validation of analytical methods. They help in verifying the performance and accuracy of instruments such as titrators, spectrophotometers, and chromatographs.

3. **Regulatory Compliance**: The use of primary and secondary standards is often mandated by regulatory bodies to ensure the quality and safety of pharmaceutical products. Accurate standardization of solutions ensures compliance with pharmacopeial standards and regulatory guidelines.

4. **Quality Control**: In the pharmaceutical industry, maintaining the quality of raw materials, intermediates, and finished products is critical. Primary and secondary standards play a vital role in quality control processes by providing accurate measurements and ensuring that products meet specified quality criteria.

Applications of Primary and Secondary Standards:

1. **Titration**: In volumetric analysis, primary and secondary standards are used to prepare standard solutions for titrations. For example, sodium carbonate is used to standardize hydrochloric acid, which can then be used to determine the concentration of an unknown acidic solution.

2. **Instrument Calibration**: Standards are used to calibrate analytical instruments, ensuring that they provide accurate measurements. For instance, a primary standard like potassium hydrogen phthalate may be used to calibrate a pH meter.

3. **Preparation of Standard Solutions**: In various analytical techniques, standard solutions of known concentration are required. Primary standards provide the basis for preparing these solutions, which are used in assays, quality control tests, and method validation.

4. **Quality Assurance in Pharmaceuticals**: The pharmaceutical industry relies heavily on primary and secondary standards for the quality assurance of drugs. Accurate standardization ensures that the active pharmaceutical ingredients (APIs) and excipients in drug formulations meet required specifications.

5. **Research and Development**: In pharmaceutical research, primary and secondary standards are used to develop and validate new analytical methods. They help in the accurate measurement of new compounds and in studying their properties and behaviors.

Concentration Unit	Definition	Formula
Molarity (M)	Number of moles of solute per liter of solution.	$M = \frac{\text{moles of solute}}{\text{liters of solution}}$
Normality (N)	Number of equivalents of solute per liter of solution.	$N = \frac{\text{equivalents of solute}}{\text{liters of solution}}$
Percent Composition	Mass of solute per 100 parts of solution (by mass or volume).	$\%(w/w) = \frac{\text{mass of solute}}{\text{total mass}} \times 100$ \n $\%(v/v) = \frac{\text{volume of solute}}{\text{total volume}} \times 100$
Parts per Million (PPM)	Mass of solute per million parts of solution (by mass).	$PPM = \frac{\text{mass of solute}}{\text{total mass}} \times 10^6$
Parts per Billion (PPB)	Mass of solute per billion parts of solution (by mass).	$PPB = \frac{\text{mass of solute}}{\text{total mass}} \times 10^9$

Methods of Expressing Concentration

TWO

VOLUMETRIC ANALYSIS

2.1 Introduction to Volumetric Analysis

2.1.1 Definition and Principles

Volumetric analysis, also known as titrimetric analysis, is a quantitative analytical technique used to determine the concentration of an analyte by measuring the volume of a standard solution (the titrant) required to react completely with the analyte. This method relies on the precise measurement of volumes and the stoichiometric relationships between reactants.

The key principle of volumetric analysis is the reaction between the analyte and the titrant, which proceeds to completion according to a known stoichiometric ratio. The endpoint of the titration, where the reaction is complete, is usually indicated by a color change of an indicator or by reaching a specific instrumental measurement (e.g., pH meter, conductivity meter).

Steps in Volumetric Analysis:

1. **Preparation of the Standard Solution**: The titrant, a solution of known concentration, is prepared accurately. This standard solution must be stable and react completely with the analyte.
2. **Sample Preparation**: The sample containing the analyte is prepared and placed in a titration vessel.
3. **Titration Process**: The titrant is added gradually to the analyte solution until the endpoint is reached. The volume of titrant used is measured precisely.
4. **Detection of Endpoint**: The endpoint is detected using an appropriate method, such as an indicator that changes color at the endpoint or an instrumental method like potentiometry.

5. **Calculation**: The concentration of the analyte is calculated using the volume of titrant added and the stoichiometry of the reaction.

Example Calculation: If a 0.1 M solution of hydrochloric acid (HCl) is titrated against a sodium hydroxide (NaOH) solution, and it takes 25 mL of HCl to neutralize 50 mL of NaOH, the concentration of NaOH can be calculated using the formula:

$C_1 V_1 = C_2 V_2$

Where C_1 and V_1 are the concentration and volume of the titrant (HCl), and C_2 and V_2 are the concentration and volume of the analyte (NaOH).

2.1.2 Types of Volumetric Analysis

Volumetric analysis encompasses several types, each based on the nature of the reaction between the titrant and the analyte:

Acid-Base Titration: This type involves the reaction between an acid and a base. The endpoint is typically indicated by a pH-sensitive indicator that changes color at the endpoint.

- **Example**: Titration of hydrochloric acid (HCl) with sodium hydroxide (NaOH).

Redox Titration: This involves a reduction-oxidation reaction between the titrant and the analyte. The endpoint can be detected using an indicator that changes color due to oxidation or reduction, or by using potentiometric methods.

- **Example**: Titration of potassium permanganate ($KMnO_4$) with oxalic acid ($C_2H_2O_4$).

Complexometric Titration: This involves the formation of a complex between the titrant and the analyte. The endpoint is usually indicated by a metal ion indicator that changes color when all the analyte has formed a complex with the titrant.

- **Example**: Titration of calcium ions (Ca^{2+}) with EDTA (ethylenediaminetetraacetic acid).

Precipitation Titration: This involves a reaction where an insoluble precipitate forms. The endpoint is detected by the formation of a visible precipitate or by using an appropriate indicator.

- **Example**: Titration of silver nitrate ($AgNO_3$) with sodium chloride (NaCl), where silver chloride (AgCl) precipitates.

Non-Aqueous Titration: This is used for titrations involving analytes or titrants that are insoluble or unstable in water. Organic solvents are used instead.

- **Example**: Titration of weak bases or acids in non-aqueous solvents such as acetic acid.

Back Titration: This involves adding an excess of a standard solution to the analyte, and then titrating the remaining excess with another standard solution. This method is used when the analyte reacts slowly or the endpoint is difficult to detect.

- **Example**: Determination of calcium carbonate ($CaCO_3$) in a sample by adding an excess of hydrochloric acid (HCl) and then titrating the remaining acid with sodium hydroxide (NaOH).

Each type of volumetric analysis is tailored to specific kinds of reactions and analytes, allowing for precise and accurate determination of concentrations in various chemical and pharmaceutical contexts.

2.2 Preparation and Standardization of Solutions

2.2.1 Oxalic Acid

Oxalic Acid is commonly used as a primary standard in titrations due to its high purity and stability. To prepare and standardize an oxalic acid solution, follow these steps:

Preparation:

1. **Weighing the Oxalic Acid**: Accurately weigh a specific amount of oxalic acid dihydrate ($H_2C_2O_4 \cdot 2H_2O$). For instance, to prepare a 0.1 M solution, weigh approximately 6.3 grams of oxalic acid dihydrate.
2. **Dissolving in Water**: Dissolve the weighed oxalic acid in a small amount of distilled water in a beaker. Stir until completely dissolved.
3. **Transferring to a Volumetric Flask**: Transfer the solution to a 1-liter volumetric flask. Rinse the beaker with distilled water and add the

rinsing to the volumetric flask to ensure all oxalic acid is transferred.

4. **Diluting to Volume**: Add distilled water to the volumetric flask until the bottom of the meniscus is at the 1-liter mark. Mix thoroughly by inverting the flask several times.

Standardization:

1. **Preparation of Sodium Hydroxide Solution**: Prepare approximately 0.1 M sodium hydroxide (NaOH) solution to standardize the oxalic acid. This can be done by dissolving about 4 grams of NaOH pellets in water and diluting to 1 liter.
2. **Titration Setup**: Fill a burette with the NaOH solution. Pipette out a measured volume (e.g., 25 mL) of the oxalic acid solution into a conical flask. Add a few drops of phenolphthalein indicator to the flask. The solution will remain colorless.
3. **Titration Procedure**: Slowly add the NaOH solution from the burette to the oxalic acid solution, swirling continuously, until a faint pink color persists for at least 30 seconds. This indicates the endpoint.

$$H_2C_2O_4 + 2NaOH \rightarrow Na_2C_2O_4 + 2H_2O$$

2.2.2 Sodium Hydroxide

Sodium Hydroxide (NaOH) is a strong base commonly used in titrations. It is often prepared and standardized against a primary standard like potassium hydrogen phthalate (KHP).

Preparation:

1. **Weighing the NaOH**: Accurately weigh approximately 4 grams of NaOH pellets.
2. **Dissolving in Water**: Dissolve the NaOH pellets in a small amount of distilled water in a beaker. Stir until completely dissolved.
3. **Transferring to a Volumetric Flask**: Transfer the solution to a 1-litre volumetric flask. Rinse the beaker with distilled water and add the rinsing to the volumetric flask.
4. **Diluting to Volume**: Add distilled water to the volumetric flask until the bottom of the meniscus is at the 1-liter mark. Mix thoroughly.

Standardization:

1. **Preparation of Potassium Hydrogen Phthalate Solution**: Accurately weigh a specific amount of KHP (approximately 2.04 grams to make a 0.1 M solution) and dissolve in distilled water. Transfer to a 1-litre volumetric flask and dilute to volume.
2. **Titration Setup**: Fill a burette with the NaOH solution. Pipette out a measured volume (e.g., 25 mL) of the KHP solution into a conical flask. Add a few drops of phenolphthalein indicator. The solution will remain colorless.
3. **Titration Procedure**: Slowly add the NaOH solution from the burette to the KHP solution, swirling continuously, until a faint pink color persists.

$$C_8H_5KO_4 + NaOH \rightarrow C_8H_5NaO_4 + H_2O$$

2.2.3 Hydrochloric Acid

Hydrochloric Acid (HCl) is a strong acid frequently used in titrations. It is usually standardized using a primary standard such as sodium carbonate (Na_2CO_3).

Preparation:

1. **Measuring the HCl**: Measure a specific volume of concentrated HCl using a pipette or burette. For example, to prepare a 0.1 M solution, use approximately 8.3 mL of concentrated HCl (which is about 37% HCl by weight).
2. **Diluting in Water**: Add the measured HCl to a 1-liter volumetric flask containing some distilled water. Be sure to add acid to water, not water to acid, to avoid splashing and excessive heat generation.
3. **Diluting to Volume**: Add distilled water to the volumetric flask until the bottom of the meniscus is at the 1-litre mark. Mix thoroughly by inverting the flask.

Standardization:

1. **Preparation of Sodium Carbonate Solution**: Accurately weigh approximately 2.65 grams of anhydrous sodium carbonate and dissolve in distilled water. Transfer to a 1-liter volumetric flask and dilute to volume.
2. **Titration Setup**: Fill a burette with the HCl solution. Pipette out a measured volume (e.g., 25 mL) of the sodium carbonate solution into a conical flask. Add a few drops of methyl orange indicator. The solution

will turn yellow.

3. **Titration Procedure**: Slowly add the HCl solution from the burette to the sodium carbonate solution, swirling continuously, until the solution changes from yellow to a faint pink-orange color.

$$Na_2CO_3 + 2HCl \rightarrow 2NaCl + H_2O + CO_2$$

2.2 Preparation and Standardization of Solutions

2.2.4 Sodium Thiosulphate

Sodium Thiosulphate ($Na_2S_2O_3$) is commonly used in iodometric titrations. To prepare and standardize a sodium thiosulphate solution, follow these steps:

Preparation of Sodium Thiosulphate Solution:

1. **Accurately weigh** approximately 24.8 grams of sodium thiosulphate pentahydrate ($Na_2S_2O_3 \cdot 5H2O$).
2. **Dissolve** the weighed sodium thiosulphate in distilled water.
3. **Transfer** the solution to a 1-liter volumetric flask.
4. **Dilute** to volume with distilled water and mix thoroughly.

Standardization of Sodium Thiosulphate Solution:

1. **Preparation of Potassium Dichromate Solution:**

   - Accurately weigh a specific amount of primary standard potassium dichromate ($K_2Cr_2O_7$).
   - Dissolve in distilled water and transfer to a 1-liter volumetric flask.
   - Dilute to volume with distilled water.

2. **Titration Setup:**

   - Fill a burette with the sodium thiosulphate solution.
   - Pipette a measured volume (e.g., 25 mL) of the potassium dichromate solution into a conical flask.
   - Add 2 grams of potassium iodide (KI) and 5 mL of dilute sulfuric acid (H_2SO_4). The solution will turn brown due to the liberation of iodine.

3. **Titration Procedure:**

- ○ Slowly add the sodium thiosulphate solution from the burette to the flask, swirling continuously, until the brown color fades to a pale yellow.
- ○ Add a few drops of starch indicator, which will turn the solution blue-black.
- ○ Continue titrating until the blue-black color disappears.

Reduction of Dichromate and Liberation of Iodine:

$K_2Cr_2O_7+14H_2SO_4+6KI\rightarrow3I_2+2Cr_2(SO_4)_3+7H_2O+6K_2SO_4$

Titration of Iodine with Sodium Thiosulphate:

$I2+2Na_2S_2O_3\rightarrow2NaI+Na_2S_4O_6$

2.2.5 Sulphuric Acid

Sulphuric Acid (H_2SO_4) is a strong acid used in various titrations. It is typically standardized using a primary standard such as sodium carbonate.

Preparation:

1. **Measuring the H_2SO_4:** Measure a specific volume of concentrated sulfuric acid using a pipette or burette. For example, to prepare a 0.1 M solution, use approximately 5.4 mL of concentrated H_2SO_4 (which is about 98% H_2SO_4 by weight).
2. **Diluting in Water:** Add the measured H_2SO_4 to a 1-liter volumetric flask containing some distilled water. Be sure to add acid to water, not water to acid, to avoid splashing and excessive heat generation.
3. **Diluting to Volume:** Add distilled water to the volumetric flask until the bottom of the meniscus is at the 1-liter mark. Mix thoroughly.

Standardization:

1. **Preparation of Sodium Carbonate Solution:** Accurately weigh approximately 2.65 grams of anhydrous sodium carbonate and dissolve in distilled water. Transfer to a 1-liter volumetric flask and dilute to volume.
2. **Titration Setup:** Fill a burette with the H_2SO_4 solution. Pipette a measured volume (e.g., 25 mL) of the sodium carbonate solution into a conical flask. Add a few drops of methyl orange indicator. The solution will turn yellow.
3. **Titration Procedure:** Slowly add the H_2SO_4 solution from the burette to the sodium carbonate solution, swirling continuously, until the solution

changes from yellow to a faint pink-orange color.

$$Na_2CO_3 + H_2SO_4 \rightarrow Na_2SO_4 + H_2O + CO_2$$

2.2.6 Potassium Permanganate

Potassium Permanganate (KMnO4) is a strong oxidizing agent used in redox titrations. It is typically standardized using a primary standard such as oxalic acid.

Preparation:

1. **Weighing the KMnO4**: Accurately weigh about 3.16 grams of potassium permanganate.
2. **Dissolving in Water**: Dissolve the weighed potassium permanganate in a small amount of distilled water in a beaker. Stir until completely dissolved.
3. **Transferring to a Volumetric Flask**: Transfer the solution to a 1-liter volumetric flask. Rinse the beaker with distilled water and add the rinsing to the volumetric flask.
4. **Diluting to Volume**: Add distilled water to the volumetric flask until the bottom of the meniscus is at the 1-liter mark. Mix thoroughly.

Standardization:

1. **Preparation of Oxalic Acid Solution**: Accurately weigh about 6.3 grams of oxalic acid dihydrate and dissolve in distilled water. Transfer to a 1-liter volumetric flask and dilute to volume.
2. **Titration Setup**: Fill a burette with the potassium permanganate solution. Pipette a measured volume (e.g., 25 mL) of the oxalic acid solution into a conical flask. Add 25 mL of dilute sulfuric acid (H_2SO_4) and heat to about 70°C.
3. **Titration Procedure**: Slowly add the potassium permanganate solution from the burette to the oxalic acid solution, swirling continuously, until the pink color persists for 30 seconds.

$$2KMnO_4 + 5H_2C_2O_4 + 3H_2SO_4 \rightarrow K_2SO_4 + 2MnSO_4 + 10CO_2 + 8H_2O$$

2.2.7 Ceric Ammonium Sulphate

Ceric Ammonium Sulphate (Ce (NH$_4$)$_4$(SO$_4$)$_4$) is a strong oxidizing agent used in redox titrations. It is typically standardized using a primary standard such as arsenic trioxide.

Preparation:

1. **Weighing the Ceric Ammonium Sulphate**: Accurately weigh about 6.62 grams of ceric ammonium sulphate.
2. **Dissolving in Water**: Dissolve the weighed ceric ammonium sulphate in a small amount of distilled water in a beaker. Add a few drops of sulfuric acid (H_2SO_4) to stabilize the solution. Stir until completely dissolved.
3. **Transferring to a Volumetric Flask**: Transfer the solution to a 1-liter volumetric flask. Rinse the beaker with distilled water and add the rinsing to the volumetric flask.
4. **Diluting to Volume**: Add distilled water to the volumetric flask until the bottom of the meniscus is at the 1-liter mark. Mix thoroughly.

Standardization:

1. **Preparation of Arsenic Trioxide Solution**: Accurately weigh about 0.495 grams of arsenic trioxide (As_2O_3) and dissolve in 50 mL of 2 M sodium hydroxide (NaOH). Add distilled water to make up to 250 mL in a volumetric flask. Acidify with dilute sulfuric acid and add a few drops of osmic acid.
2. **Titration Setup**: Fill a burette with the ceric ammonium sulphate solution. Pipette a measured volume (e.g., 25 mL) of the arsenic trioxide solution into a conical flask. Add 25 mL of 3 M sulfuric acid.
3. **Titration Procedure**: Slowly add the ceric ammonium sulphate solution from the burette to the arsenic trioxide solution, swirling continuously, until the yellow color changes to a slight pink.

$$As_2O_3 + 2Ce\,(NH_4)_4(SO_4)_4 + 5H_2SO_4 \rightarrow 2Ce\,(SO_4) + (NH_4)_2SO_4 + 5H_2O + 2As\,(OH)_3$$

THREE

ERRORS IN PHARMACEUTICAL ANALYSIS

3.1 Types of Errors

3.1.1 Systematic Errors

Systematic Errors are consistent and repeatable errors that occur due to flaws in equipment, experimental design, or procedure. These errors cause measurements to be consistently biased in one direction, either too high or too low. Systematic errors can be further categorized into three main types: instrumental errors, methodological errors, and personal errors.

Instrumental Errors: These arise from imperfections or malfunctions in the measuring instruments. For instance, a balance that is not calibrated correctly will consistently give incorrect mass readings. Similarly, a spectrophotometer with a faulty wavelength setting will produce inaccurate absorbance readings. Regular maintenance and calibration of instruments are essential to minimize these errors.

Methodological Errors: These occur due to improper experimental design or procedural flaws. For example, using an inappropriate indicator in a titration can lead to a systematic deviation in the endpoint detection. Another common source of methodological error is incorrect sampling techniques, which can lead to unrepresentative samples and biased results. Ensuring rigorous experimental protocols and adhering to standardized procedures can help reduce methodological errors.

Personal Errors: These are caused by the experimenter's biases, carelessness, or lack of experience. For instance, consistently reading the meniscus from the top instead of the bottom can lead to systematic volume measurement errors. Personal errors can be minimized through proper training, experience, and attention to detail.

Systematic errors can be identified and corrected by comparing measurements with known standards or by using alternative methods. For example, if a systematic error is suspected in a balance, calibrating the balance with known weights can help identify and correct the error. Similarly, cross-validating results with different analytical methods can help detect and eliminate systematic biases.

Example: Suppose a balance is consistently giving readings that are 0.5 grams higher than the true value. If a series of measurements are taken using this balance, all results will be systematically higher by 0.5 grams. By calibrating the balance and correcting for this offset, the systematic error can be eliminated.

3.1.2 Random Errors

Random Errors are unpredictable and occur due to inherent fluctuations in the measurement process. Unlike systematic errors, random errors cause measurements to vary in an unpredictable manner, leading to scatter around the true value. These errors arise from a multitude of sources, such as environmental changes, observer variations, and limitations of measuring instruments.

Environmental Changes: Factors such as temperature, humidity, and atmospheric pressure can cause random fluctuations in measurements. For example, slight changes in room temperature can affect the density of a liquid, leading to variability in volume measurements. Controlling environmental conditions as much as possible and conducting measurements in a controlled environment can help minimize random errors.

Observer Variations: Human factors, such as differences in perception and reaction time, contribute to random errors. For instance, different observers might read the same measurement slightly differently due to variations in visual acuity or interpretation of instrument scales. Ensuring that measurements are taken by the same person or using automated instruments can reduce observer-related random errors.

Instrument Limitations: The precision of measuring instruments inherently limits the accuracy of measurements. For example, a digital balance with a readability of 0.01 grams will have small random fluctuations in readings within that limit. Using instruments with higher precision and ensuring proper maintenance can help reduce these errors.

Random errors are typically assessed and quantified using statistical methods. Repeated measurements of the same quantity can help estimate the magnitude of random errors. The standard deviation is a common statistical measure used to quantify the spread of measurements due to random errors. By averaging multiple measurements, the effect of random errors can be minimized, leading to a more accurate estimate of the true value.

Example: Suppose the mass of an object is measured multiple times using a balance, and the readings vary slightly due to random fluctuations. The individual measurements might be 5.01 grams, 5.03 grams, 5.00 grams, and 5.02 grams. These variations are random errors. Calculating the average of these measurements and the standard deviation provides an estimate of the true mass and the degree of random error.

Minimizing Random Errors: While it is impossible to eliminate random errors entirely, their impact can be minimized by:

- Conducting multiple measurements and using the average value.
- Ensuring consistent experimental conditions.
- Using high-precision instruments.
- Training personnel to reduce observer-related variations.

3.2 Sources of Errors
3.2.1 Instrumental Errors

Instrumental Errors are deviations in measurements caused by imperfections, malfunctions, or limitations of the instruments used in analytical procedures. These errors can significantly affect the accuracy and precision of the results. Understanding the sources and types of instrumental errors is crucial for identifying and correcting them.

Types of Instrumental Errors:

1. **Calibration Errors**: Calibration errors occur when instruments are not calibrated correctly. Calibration is the process of setting an instrument to give accurate measurements by comparing it with a standard. If the calibration is off, all measurements taken with the instrument will be consistently biased. For instance, a balance that is not calibrated

correctly might consistently read 0.1 grams higher or lower than the actual weight. Regular calibration using certified standards is essential to maintain the accuracy of instruments.

2. **Zero Errors**: Zero errors happen when an instrument does not read zero when it should. For example, a balance that shows a reading of 0.05 grams when empty has a zero error. This type of error can be corrected by taring or zeroing the instrument before taking measurements.

3. **Parallax Errors**: Parallax errors occur when the reading is taken from an incorrect angle, leading to inaccurate results. This is common in instruments with analog scales, such as burettes and graduated cylinders. Ensuring that the observer's line of sight is perpendicular to the scale can minimize parallax errors.

4. **Drift**: Drift refers to gradual changes in the instrument's readings over time. This can be caused by changes in environmental conditions (such as temperature or humidity), aging of electronic components, or mechanical wear. Regular maintenance and recalibration of instruments can help reduce drift.

5. **Linearity Errors**: Linearity errors occur when the instrument's response is not directly proportional to the input across its entire range. For example, a spectrophotometer might give accurate readings at low concentrations but deviate at higher concentrations. This non-linearity can be corrected by applying a calibration curve that accounts for the instrument's behavior across its operating range.

6. **Hysteresis**: Hysteresis is the difference in the instrument's readings when the same measurement is approached from different directions. For example, a balance might show different readings when a weight is added versus when it is removed. This error can be minimized by ensuring consistent measurement procedures and allowing the instrument to stabilize between measurements.

7. **Sensitivity Errors**: Sensitivity errors occur when an instrument is not sensitive enough to detect small changes in the quantity being measured. For instance, a thermometer with a low sensitivity might not detect minor temperature fluctuations. Using instruments with appropriate sensitivity for the measurements being taken is essential to avoid this type of error.

8. **Environmental Influences**: Instruments can be affected by external environmental factors such as temperature, humidity, vibrations, and electromagnetic interference. For example, electronic balances can be

sensitive to air currents and vibrations, causing fluctuations in readings. Conducting measurements in controlled environments and using protective enclosures can help mitigate these effects.

Examples of Instrumental Errors in Common Analytical Instruments:

- **Balances**: Calibration errors, zero errors, drift, and sensitivity errors.
- **Spectrophotometers**: Linearity errors, calibration errors, and sensitivity to environmental conditions.
- **pH Meters**: Calibration errors, drift, and temperature effects.
- **Burettes**: Parallax errors and calibration errors.

Minimizing Instrumental Errors:

1. **Regular Calibration**: Calibrate instruments regularly using certified reference materials to ensure accurate measurements.
2. **Proper Maintenance**: Perform routine maintenance and servicing of instruments to prevent malfunctions and wear.
3. **Environmental Control**: Conduct measurements in controlled environments to minimize the effects of temperature, humidity, and vibrations.
4. **Training**: Ensure that personnel are well-trained in the correct use and handling of instruments to avoid operator-induced errors.
5. **Using High-Quality Instruments**: Invest in high-quality, reliable instruments that have low susceptibility to errors and environmental influences.

Example of Calibration Procedure for a Balance:

1. **Prepare Calibration Weights**: Use certified weights that are traceable to national standards.
2. **Zero the Balance**: Ensure the balance reads zero with no load.
3. **Place Calibration Weight**: Place the calibration weight on the balance and record the reading.
4. **Adjust Calibration**: If the reading deviates from the known weight, adjust the balance according to the manufacturer's instructions.
5. **Repeat for Different Weights**: Repeat the process for different weights to ensure linearity across the balance's range.

3.2 Sources of Errors

3.2.2 Personal Errors

Personal Errors are mistakes or biases introduced by the experimenter during the measurement process. These errors can significantly affect the accuracy and reliability of analytical results. Understanding the sources and types of personal errors is essential for identifying and minimizing them.

Types of Personal Errors:

1. **Observation Errors**: Observation errors occur when the experimenter misreads the measurement due to poor vision, incorrect reading angle, or distractions. For instance, reading the meniscus of a liquid at an angle rather than at eye level can lead to parallax errors, resulting in incorrect volume measurements. Ensuring proper lighting, minimizing distractions, and consistently reading measurements at eye level can help reduce observation errors.

2. **Interpretation Errors**: These errors happen when the experimenter incorrectly interprets the measurement or the procedure. For example, misinterpreting the color change of an indicator during a titration can lead to an inaccurate determination of the endpoint. Thorough training and experience in interpreting measurement results and experimental procedures are crucial for minimizing interpretation errors.

3. **Technique Errors**: Technique errors arise from improper handling or use of equipment and instruments. Examples include incorrect pipetting techniques, inconsistent mixing of solutions, or improper calibration of instruments. Standardizing techniques through training and following standard operating procedures (SOPs) can help reduce technique errors.

4. **Recording Errors**: Recording errors occur when data is incorrectly transcribed or documented. For example, writing down the wrong number or unit can lead to significant errors in data analysis. Double-checking entries, using digital data recording systems, and maintaining accurate lab notebooks can help prevent recording errors.

5. **Calculation Errors**: These errors happen when the experimenter makes mistakes in mathematical calculations. This can include errors in arithmetic, incorrect use of formulas, or incorrect conversion of units. Using calculators or software for calculations and verifying results through cross-checking can help minimize calculation errors.

6. **Bias**: Personal bias can affect the measurement process, consciously or unconsciously. For example, expecting a certain result can influence the

experimenter's reading of an instrument. Maintaining objectivity and using blinded or automated methods can help reduce bias.

7. **Fatigue and Distraction**: Experimenter fatigue and distractions can lead to mistakes. Long hours in the lab without breaks or interruptions during critical measurements can cause errors. Ensuring adequate rest, taking regular breaks, and minimizing distractions during experiments are important to maintain accuracy.

Examples of Personal Errors in Common Analytical Procedures:

- **Titrations**: Misreading the endpoint due to incorrect interpretation of the color change.
- **Weighing**: Inaccurate reading of the balance due to parallax errors or not zeroing the balance before use.
- **Pipetting**: Inconsistent volume measurements due to improper pipetting techniques, such as not expelling the full volume or introducing air bubbles.
- **Data Recording**: Writing down incorrect measurements or misplacing decimal points.

Minimizing Personal Errors:

1. **Training and Practice**: Regular training and practice in using analytical techniques and instruments correctly are essential. Familiarity with the procedures and equipment reduces the likelihood of errors.
2. **Standard Operating Procedures (SOPs)**: Following well-documented SOPs ensures consistency and accuracy in experimental procedures.
3. **Double-Checking**: Implementing a system of double-checking measurements, calculations, and data entries can catch errors before they affect the results.
4. **Automation**: Using automated systems for measurements and data recording can significantly reduce personal errors. Automated titrators, digital balances, and computerized data acquisition systems minimize human intervention and associated errors.
5. **Maintaining Focus**: Ensuring a focused and distraction-free environment during critical measurements. Taking regular breaks and avoiding long hours of continuous work helps maintain accuracy.

6. **Proper Documentation**: Maintaining detailed and accurate lab notebooks and records. Documenting procedures, observations, and results meticulously helps in tracking and verifying data.

Example of Minimizing Personal Errors in a Titration Procedure:

1. **Preparation**: Ensure all reagents and equipment are prepared and calibrated correctly. Familiarize yourself with the procedure and endpoint indicators.
2. **Consistent Technique**: Use a consistent technique for adding the titrant, such as adding drops slowly near the endpoint and swirling the solution continuously.
3. **Reading the Meniscus**: Always read the meniscus at eye level to avoid parallax errors.
4. **Using Indicators**: Use appropriate indicators and be consistent in interpreting the color change. Consider using a pH meter for more precise endpoint determination.
5. **Recording Data**: Record all measurements immediately and double-check entries for accuracy. Use digital recording systems if available.

In summary, personal errors can significantly impact the accuracy and reliability of analytical results. Identifying and minimizing these errors through proper training, consistent techniques, careful observation, and accurate documentation are essential for ensuring the integrity of analytical data. By adopting best practices and leveraging automation, personal errors can be significantly reduced, leading to more reliable and reproducible results in pharmaceutical analysis.

3.2 Sources of Errors

3.2.3 Method Errors

Method Errors refer to inaccuracies that arise from the procedures used to conduct experiments or measurements. These errors can stem from the inherent limitations of the analytical methods, improper application of techniques, or outdated protocols. Understanding and addressing method errors is essential for ensuring the reliability and accuracy of experimental results.

Types of Method Errors:

1. **Inadequate Method Development**: This occurs when the analytical method is not adequately developed or optimized for the specific analysis. For instance, using a detection method that is not sensitive enough for the analyte's expected concentration levels can lead to undetected or underestimated amounts.

2. **Improper Method Selection**: Choosing an inappropriate method for the analysis can lead to significant errors. For example, selecting a non-specific assay method that reacts with multiple components in a sample can provide misleading results about the concentration of the target analyte.

3. **Incorrect Implementation**: Even if the chosen method is appropriate, incorrect implementation of the method can introduce errors. This includes inaccuracies in sample preparation, incorrect operational settings on instruments, or failure to follow the defined procedural steps accurately.

4. **Lack of Robustness**: A method may not be robust if small changes in environmental conditions or slight variations in reagent quality affect the results significantly. For example, a method that gives different results under slightly different temperatures or with reagents from different suppliers lacks robustness.

5. **Inadequate Method Validation**: Method validation is crucial to ensure that an analytical method is suitable for its intended purpose. Insufficient validation can lead to method errors when the method's reliability has not been adequately tested across its full range of intended conditions.

Examples of Method Errors in Common Analytical Procedures:

- **Chromatography**: Using an incorrect mobile phase composition or flow rate can lead to poor separation of components, affecting the accuracy of quantitation.
- **Spectroscopy**: Not accounting for sample turbidity or fluorescence when using UV-Visible spectroscopy can interfere with absorbance readings.
- **Titration**: Using an indicator with an inappropriate color change range relative to the analyte's pH change can result in a misidentified endpoint.
- **Sample Preparation**: Inadequate mixing, incorrect sample size, or contamination during sample preparation can lead to unrepresentative or altered sample characteristics.

Minimizing Method Errors:

1. **Thorough Method Development and Optimization**: Invest time in developing and optimizing methods specifically tailored to the analysis requirements. This includes selecting the most appropriate technique, determining optimal operational parameters, and validating these choices through pilot studies.
2. **Rigorous Method Validation**: Validate methods rigorously to ensure accuracy, precision, sensitivity, specificity, and robustness. Validation should include assessments under different conditions to understand the method's limitations and performance boundaries.
3. **Standard Operating Procedures (SOPs)**: Develop and adhere to detailed SOPs that outline every step of the analytical procedure. SOPs help standardize operations and reduce variability introduced by different operators or different experimental sessions.
4. **Regular Training**: Ensure that all personnel are trained in the specific methods they are implementing. Regular training sessions can update team members on the latest techniques and reinforce the importance of precision and adherence to protocols.
5. **Quality Control Checks**: Implement quality control checks and use control samples to monitor the consistency and accuracy of the analytical methods. Regular checks help identify and correct deviations from expected outcomes before they impact the analysis results.
6. **Continuous Improvement**: Encourage a culture of continuous improvement where methods are regularly reviewed and updated based on the latest scientific developments and internal findings. This adaptive approach can help minimize method errors by ensuring that the procedures remain state-of-the-art and fully functional.

Example of Addressing Method Errors in HPLC Analysis:

1. **Method Optimization**: Carefully select the column, mobile phase, and gradient conditions based on the chemical properties of the analytes. Perform preliminary runs to optimize these parameters for peak resolution and retention times.
2. **Validation**: Validate the HPLC method for accuracy, precision, linearity, limit of detection, and robustness. Perform validation under different conditions, such as different operator shifts and different instrument

setups.

3. **SOPs and Training**: Develop comprehensive SOPs for the HPLC procedure and ensure all operators are trained to perform the analysis consistently. Include troubleshooting guidelines for common issues like peak tailing or unexpected retention times.

4. **Quality Control**: Use quality control samples in each batch of analyses to monitor method performance. Establish criteria for acceptable control results and investigate any deviations.

3.2 Sources of Errors
3.2.4 Environmental Factors

Environmental Factors can significantly influence the accuracy and reliability of analytical measurements. These factors include temperature, humidity, air currents, light, and electromagnetic interference. Understanding how these environmental conditions affect analytical procedures and implementing strategies to mitigate their impact is crucial for obtaining precise and accurate results.

Types of Environmental Factors:

1. **Temperature Variations**: Temperature fluctuations can affect the physical and chemical properties of samples and reagents. For instance, changes in temperature can alter the density and viscosity of liquids, which in turn affects volumetric measurements. Temperature can also influence the reaction rates and stability of chemical compounds.

Example: In a titration, temperature variations can cause expansion or contraction of the liquid, leading to incorrect volume measurements. Conducting the titration at a consistent temperature and using temperature-controlled environments can help minimize this error.

1. **Humidity Levels**: Humidity can affect hygroscopic materials, causing them to absorb or lose water, which changes their mass. High humidity levels can also impact the performance of electronic instruments and lead to condensation issues.

Example: Powders and solid reagents that are hygroscopic can gain weight when exposed to high humidity, leading to inaccuracies in mass measurements. Using desiccators for storing hygroscopic substances and controlling humidity levels in the laboratory can help mitigate this issue.

3. **Air Currents and Vibration**: Air currents and vibrations can affect sensitive instruments such as balances and spectrophotometers. Even slight movements or drafts can cause fluctuations in readings.

   Example: Analytical balances are highly sensitive to air currents and vibrations, which can lead to unstable readings. Placing the balance in a draft-free, stable environment and using anti-vibration tables can reduce these effects.

4. **Light Exposure**: Light, especially UV and visible light, can cause photodegradation of light-sensitive samples. Prolonged exposure to light can alter the chemical composition and concentration of analytes.

   Example: Many pharmaceutical compounds are sensitive to light and can degrade when exposed. Using amber-colored glassware or opaque containers and minimizing exposure to light during sample preparation and analysis can help protect light-sensitive substances.

5. **Electromagnetic Interference**: Electromagnetic fields from nearby electronic devices can interfere with the operation of sensitive instruments such as spectrophotometers and chromatographs. This interference can lead to noise and inaccurate readings.

   Example: Electromagnetic interference can affect the baseline stability of a spectrophotometer, resulting in noisy or drifted absorbance readings. Shielding the instruments from electromagnetic sources and using proper grounding techniques can minimize these effects.

6. **Contaminants in the Environment**: Dust, fumes, and other airborne contaminants can settle on samples or interfere with instrument readings. This can lead to inaccuracies in measurements and analytical results.

   Example: Dust particles can interfere with the light path in a spectrophotometer, affecting the accuracy of absorbance measurements. Maintaining a clean laboratory environment and using dust covers for sensitive equipment can help prevent contamination.

Minimizing the Impact of Environmental Factors:

1. **Controlled Environments**: Conduct experiments in temperature and humidity-controlled environments to minimize fluctuations. Laboratories with climate control systems can maintain consistent conditions, reducing the impact of environmental variations on measurements.
2. **Proper Storage**: Store sensitive reagents and samples in appropriate conditions. Use desiccators for hygroscopic substances, amber-colored glassware for light-sensitive compounds, and airtight containers to prevent contamination.
3. **Stable Work Surfaces**: Use anti-vibration tables and place sensitive instruments on stable surfaces away from sources of vibrations and drafts. This helps ensure stable and accurate readings from instruments like balances and spectrophotometers.
4. **Shielding and Grounding**: Protect instruments from electromagnetic interference by proper shielding and grounding. Place sensitive equipment away from sources of electromagnetic fields and use grounding techniques to reduce interference.
5. **Regular Calibration and Maintenance**: Regularly calibrate instruments to account for any environmental influences. Routine maintenance ensures that instruments are functioning correctly and are less susceptible to environmental variations.
6. **Standard Operating Procedures (SOPs)**: Develop and follow SOPs that include guidelines for controlling environmental conditions. This ensures consistency in experimental procedures and minimizes the impact of environmental factors on results.

Example of Mitigating Environmental Factors in Spectrophotometric Analysis:

1. **Temperature Control**: Perform spectrophotometric measurements in a temperature-controlled room to ensure consistent absorbance readings.
2. **Light Protection**: Use amber-colored cuvettes and minimize exposure of samples to light during preparation and analysis to prevent photodegradation.

3. **Clean Environment**: Ensure the spectrophotometer is placed in a clean area, free from dust and other contaminants. Use dust covers when the instrument is not in use.
4. **Calibration**: Regularly calibrate the spectrophotometer using standard reference materials to account for any drift or baseline noise.

3.3 Methods to Minimize Errors
3.3.1 Calibration and Standardization

Calibration and standardization are essential practices in analytical chemistry to ensure the accuracy, precision, and reliability of measurement instruments and methods. These processes involve comparing the measurement from an instrument or method against a known standard to detect and correct any deviations. Regular calibration and standardization help minimize errors and maintain the integrity of analytical results.

Calibration: Calibration is the process of adjusting and verifying the accuracy of measurement instruments by comparing their outputs with a known standard. The goal of calibration is to identify and correct any discrepancies between the instrument's readings and the true value.

Standardization: Standardization involves establishing a reference point or standard against which measurements can be compared. This is particularly important in titrations and other quantitative analyses where accurate concentration measurements are crucial.

Importance of Calibration and Standardization:

- **Accuracy**: Ensures that the instrument or method provides correct results.
- **Precision**: Ensures that repeated measurements under unchanged conditions provide consistent results.
- **Traceability**: Provides a clear record of how measurements are linked to recognized standards.
- **Compliance**: Meets regulatory and quality control requirements.

Steps for Effective Calibration:

1. **Identify Calibration Requirements**:

   - Determine which instruments and methods require calibration.

- Identify the frequency of calibration based on the instrument's usage and manufacturer's recommendations.

2. **Select Appropriate Standards**:

- Use primary standards or certified reference materials with known and high accuracy.
- Ensure that standards are traceable to national or international standards.

3. **Perform Calibration**:

- Clean and prepare the instrument according to the manufacturer's instructions.
- Measure the known standard and record the instrument's reading.
- Adjust the instrument to match the standard if there is a deviation.
- Repeat the measurement to ensure consistency and accuracy.

4. **Document Calibration**:

- Record the calibration data, including the date, instrument identification, standard used, and any adjustments made.
- Maintain a calibration log for traceability and future reference.

5. **Regular Maintenance and Recalibration**:

- Perform regular maintenance on instruments to ensure they remain in good working condition.
- Recalibrate instruments at regular intervals and after any major maintenance or repair.

Example of Calibration Procedure for a pH Meter:

1. **Preparation**:

- Clean the pH meter electrode with distilled water and gently blot it dry with a lint-free tissue.
- Ensure the pH meter is at room temperature and stable.

2. **Calibration Solutions**:

   - Use pH buffer solutions with known values (e.g., pH 4.00, pH 7.00, and pH 10.00).
   - Ensure the buffer solutions are fresh and at the same temperature as the pH meter.

3. **Calibration Process**:

   - Immerse the electrode in the pH 7.00 buffer solution and allow the reading to stabilize.
   - Adjust the pH meter to read exactly 7.00 if necessary.
   - Rinse the electrode with distilled water and repeat the process with the pH 4.00 and pH 10.00 buffer solutions.
   - Adjust the meter if needed to match the known values of the buffer solutions.

4. **Documentation**:

   - Record the calibration data, including the buffer solutions used, the initial and adjusted readings, and the date of calibration.

Steps for Effective Standardization:

1. **Prepare Standard Solutions**:

   - Accurately weigh the primary standard substance using a calibrated balance.
   - Dissolve the substance in a suitable solvent and transfer it to a volumetric flask.
   - Dilute to the mark with solvent and mix thoroughly.

2. **Perform Titration**:

   - Pipette a measured volume of the standard solution into a titration flask.
   - Add an appropriate indicator if necessary.
   - Titrate with the titrant solution until the endpoint is reached.

3. **Calculate Concentration**:

- Use the titration data to calculate the concentration of the titrant solution.
- Apply the stoichiometric relationship between the standard and the titrant.

4. **Documentation**:

- Record the details of the standardization, including the amounts used, titration volumes, and calculated concentrations.

Example of Standardization Procedure for Sodium Hydroxide Solution:

1. **Preparation of Oxalic Acid Solution**:

- Weigh approximately 6.3 grams of oxalic acid dihydrate and dissolve in distilled water.
- Transfer the solution to a 1-liter volumetric flask and dilute to the mark with distilled water.

2. **Titration**:

- Pipette 25.0 mL of the oxalic acid solution into a conical flask.
- Add a few drops of phenolphthalein indicator.
- Titrate with the sodium hydroxide solution until a faint pink color persists for 30 seconds.

3. **Calculation**:

- Calculate the molarity of the sodium hydroxide solution using the titration data: Molarity of NaOH = (Molarity of Oxalic Acid * Volume of Oxalic Acid) / (Volume of NaOH) * 2/1

4. **Documentation**:

- Record the volumes used, the calculated concentration, and the date of standardization.

3.3 Methods to Minimize Errors
3.3.2 Proper Training and Technique

Proper training and technique are crucial in minimizing errors in analytical chemistry. Even with well-calibrated instruments and standardized methods, the accuracy and precision of results largely depend on the skill and knowledge of the personnel conducting the analysis. Proper training ensures that analysts are proficient in using the equipment and techniques correctly, while adherence to proper techniques reduces variability and enhances reproducibility.

Importance of Proper Training and Technique:

- **Accuracy**: Correct use of equipment and methods ensures that measurements reflect the true values.
- **Precision**: Consistent technique reduces variability in results, ensuring that repeated measurements are similar.
- **Safety**: Proper training minimizes the risk of accidents and exposure to hazardous substances.
- **Efficiency**: Skilled personnel can perform analyses more quickly and with fewer mistakes, improving overall productivity.

Key Aspects of Proper Training and Technique:

1. **Understanding the Theory**:

   - Analysts must understand the principles behind the techniques they are using. This includes knowledge of chemical reactions, the purpose of each step in the procedure, and the expected outcomes.
   - Training should include theoretical sessions explaining the science behind the analytical methods.

2. **Familiarization with Equipment**:

   - Analysts should be thoroughly familiar with the operation of the equipment they will be using. This includes understanding how to set up, calibrate, and troubleshoot the instruments.

- Practical training sessions should provide hands-on experience with the equipment under the supervision of experienced personnel.

3. **Standard Operating Procedures (SOPs)**:

   - Detailed SOPs should be developed for all analytical methods. These documents should outline each step of the procedure, the equipment and reagents required, safety precautions, and troubleshooting tips.
   - Analysts should be trained to follow SOPs meticulously to ensure consistency and accuracy.

4. **Precision in Measurements**:

   - Accurate pipetting, weighing, and volumetric measurements are critical. Analysts should be trained in the correct use of pipettes, balances, and volumetric flasks.
   - Techniques such as reading the meniscus at eye level, avoiding air bubbles in pipettes, and using analytical balances properly should be emphasized.

5. **Sample Preparation**:

   - Proper sample preparation is vital for obtaining reliable results. This includes correct sampling, homogenization, and avoiding contamination.
   - Training should cover best practices in sample handling and preparation to ensure representativeness and integrity of samples.

6. **Reagent Handling**:

   - Analysts should be trained in the correct handling, preparation, and storage of reagents to prevent contamination and degradation.
   - This includes labeling, proper storage conditions, and using high-purity reagents where necessary.

7. **Data Recording and Analysis**:

- ◦ Accurate data recording is essential. Analysts should be trained to record data meticulously in lab notebooks or electronic systems.
- ◦ Training should also cover basic data analysis skills, including calculating concentrations, performing statistical analyses, and interpreting results.

8. **Quality Control and Assurance**:

- ◦ Training should include quality control procedures such as using control samples, performing replicate analyses, and participating in proficiency testing.
- ◦ Understanding the importance of quality assurance and adhering to quality control measures ensures the reliability of analytical results.

Examples of Proper Training and Techniques in Common Analytical Procedures:

- **Pipetting**:

  - ◦ Use the correct pipette for the volume being measured.
  - ◦ Pre-rinse the pipette with the solution to be measured.
  - ◦ Ensure the pipette is vertical when drawing up and dispensing the liquid.
  - ◦ Avoid air bubbles by releasing the plunger slowly and smoothly.

- **Weighing**:

  - ◦ Use an analytical balance for precise measurements.
  - ◦ Calibrate the balance before use.
  - ◦ Tare the balance with the weighing container before adding the sample.
  - ◦ Avoid drafts and vibrations during weighing.

- **Titration**:

  - ◦ Standardize titrant solutions regularly.
  - ◦ Use a burette and ensure no air bubbles in the burette or the tip.

- Add titrant slowly near the endpoint while continuously swirling the flask.
- Use appropriate indicators and understand the expected color change at the endpoint.

Continuous Improvement and Refresher Training:

- Ongoing training programs should be implemented to keep analysts updated on new techniques, equipment, and best practices.
- Regular refresher courses help reinforce proper techniques and address any skill gaps.
- Encouraging a culture of continuous improvement and learning ensures that analysts remain proficient and knowledgeable.

Example of Implementing Proper Training and Technique for HPLC Analysis:

1. **Theory and Equipment Familiarization:**

   - Provide theoretical training on the principles of chromatography and the specific HPLC method being used.
   - Conduct hands-on training sessions to familiarize analysts with the HPLC instrument, including setting up columns, preparing mobile phases, and calibrating detectors.

2. **Following SOPs:**

   - Develop detailed SOPs for the HPLC method, including sample preparation, instrument setup, and data analysis.
   - Ensure analysts are trained to follow SOPs accurately and understand the importance of each step.

3. **Precision in Measurements:**

   - Train analysts in accurate pipetting and weighing techniques for preparing standard and sample solutions.
   - Emphasize the importance of avoiding contamination and maintaining clean lab environments.

4. **Quality Control**:

  ◦ Include training on the use of control samples and internal standards to monitor the performance of the HPLC method.
  ◦ Ensure analysts understand how to interpret quality control data and take corrective actions if necessary.

3.4 Accuracy, Precision, and Significant Figures
3.4.1 Definitions and Importance

Accuracy, precision, and significant figures are fundamental concepts in analytical chemistry that play a critical role in ensuring the reliability and validity of measurement results. Understanding these concepts helps analysts to achieve high-quality data and make informed decisions based on their measurements.

Accuracy: Accuracy refers to the closeness of a measured value to the true or accepted value. It indicates how correct a measurement is. High accuracy means that the measured value is very close to the true value. Accuracy is affected by systematic errors, which can be minimized through calibration, proper method selection, and thorough validation.

Importance of Accuracy:

- **Reliability**: Accurate measurements ensure that the results are reliable and can be trusted for decision-making.
- **Compliance**: Regulatory agencies require accurate data to ensure the safety and efficacy of pharmaceutical products.
- **Quality Control**: In quality control, accuracy is crucial for verifying that products meet specified standards and specifications.

Example: If the true concentration of a solution is 0.100 M and a measurement yields 0.099 M, the measurement is considered accurate because it is close to the true value.

Precision: Precision refers to the closeness of repeated measurements of the same quantity under unchanged conditions. It indicates the reproducibility of measurements. High precision means that repeated measurements give similar results. Precision is affected by random errors, which can be minimized through consistent technique, proper training, and environmental control.

Importance of Precision:

- **Consistency**: High precision ensures that results are consistent and reproducible over multiple measurements.
- **Statistical Validity**: Precise measurements provide a strong basis for statistical analysis and quality control.
- **Method Validation**: Precision is a key parameter in validating analytical methods to ensure they can consistently produce reliable results.

Example: If three measurements of a solution's concentration yield values of 0.101 M, 0.099 M, and 0.100 M, the measurements are considered precise because they are close to each other.

Significant Figures: Significant figures are the digits in a measurement that carry meaningful information about its precision. They include all known digits plus one estimated digit. The number of significant figures reflects the certainty of the measurement and helps convey the precision of the data.

Importance of Significant Figures:

- **Data Integrity**: Using the correct number of significant figures ensures that the reported data accurately reflects the precision of the measurements.
- **Communication**: Significant figures help communicate the reliability and precision of the data to others.
- **Calculation Accuracy**: In calculations, maintaining the correct number of significant figures prevents the introduction of artificial precision or error.

Rules for Determining Significant Figures:

1. **Non-Zero Digits**: All non-zero digits are significant (e.g., 123 has three significant figures).
2. **Leading Zeros**: Leading zeros are not significant (e.g., 0.0023 has two significant figures).
3. **Captive Zeros**: Zeros between non-zero digits are significant (e.g., 1002 has four significant figures).
4. **Trailing Zeros**: Trailing zeros in a decimal number are significant (e.g., 2.300 has four significant figures).

Example: If a balance reads 0.1000 g, the number 0.1000 has four significant figures, indicating the precision of the balance measurement.

Combining Accuracy, Precision, and Significant Figures: Achieving high accuracy and precision in measurements is essential for reliable analytical data. Properly reporting significant figures ensures that the data's precision is accurately communicated.

Example in Practice:

1. **Calibration**: Calibrate instruments regularly to maintain accuracy.
2. **Consistent Technique**: Use consistent techniques to achieve high precision.
3. **Recording Data**: Record data with the correct number of significant figures to reflect the measurement's precision.

Application in Analytical Chemistry:

- **Titration**: When performing a titration, the endpoint must be accurately determined (accuracy) and consistent (precision) across multiple trials. The titration results should be reported with the appropriate number of significant figures to reflect the precision of the volume measurements.
- **Spectroscopy**: In spectroscopic measurements, accurate calibration of the instrument ensures that the absorbance values reflect the true concentration of the analyte. Repeated measurements of the same sample should yield consistent absorbance values (precision), and the results should be reported with significant figures that match the instrument's precision.

3.4 Accuracy, Precision, and Significant Figures
3.4.2 Methods to Improve Accuracy and Precision

Improving the accuracy and precision of analytical measurements is essential for obtaining reliable and valid results. Various strategies and best practices can be employed to enhance both accuracy and precision in the laboratory.

Methods to Improve Accuracy:

1. **Regular Calibration**:

- **Calibrate Instruments**: Regular calibration of instruments against certified reference materials ensures that measurements are accurate. Calibration should be performed according to a fixed schedule and after any significant maintenance or repair.
- **Use Primary Standards**: Use primary standards for calibration as they are highly pure and have a well-known value.

2. **Method Validation**:

- **Validate Analytical Methods**: Ensure that analytical methods are validated for accuracy. This includes testing for linearity, accuracy, precision, specificity, and sensitivity.
- **Recovery Studies**: Perform recovery studies by spiking known quantities of analytes into the matrix and measuring the recovery rate to validate the method's accuracy.

3. **Quality Control Samples**:

- **Use Control Samples**: Regularly analyze quality control samples alongside test samples to monitor the accuracy of the analytical method.
- **Proficiency Testing**: Participate in interlaboratory proficiency testing to compare results and ensure accuracy across different laboratories.

4. **Environmental Control**:

- **Maintain Stable Conditions**: Control environmental factors such as temperature, humidity, and air currents to minimize their impact on measurements. Use temperature-controlled rooms and enclosures for sensitive measurements.
- **Protect from Light**: Shield light-sensitive samples from exposure to light to prevent degradation and ensure accurate measurements.

5. **Proper Sample Handling**:

- **Avoid Contamination**: Use clean, appropriately labeled containers and tools to prevent sample contamination. Ensure that samples are stored under suitable conditions to maintain their integrity.

- ◦ **Homogenize Samples**: Ensure samples are thoroughly mixed and homogenized to obtain representative aliquots for analysis.

6. **Instrument Maintenance**:

   - ◦ **Routine Maintenance**: Regularly maintain and service instruments to ensure they are functioning correctly. Follow the manufacturer's recommendations for maintenance schedules.
   - ◦ **Error Detection**: Implement procedures for detecting and correcting instrument errors, such as drift or malfunction.

Methods to Improve Precision:

1. **Consistent Technique**:

   - ◦ **Standardize Procedures**: Use standardized procedures and protocols to ensure consistency in measurements. This includes following detailed Standard Operating Procedures (SOPs).
   - ◦ **Training and Skill Development**: Provide regular training to analysts to ensure they are proficient in the techniques used. Skilled analysts are less likely to introduce variability.

2. **Replication and Repetition**:

   - ◦ **Multiple Measurements**: Perform multiple measurements of the same sample to assess precision. Calculate the mean and standard deviation to evaluate the consistency of the results.
   - ◦ **Replicate Analyses**: Conduct replicate analyses of samples to identify and minimize random errors.

3. **Control Environmental Factors**:

   - ◦ **Minimize Variability**: Control environmental factors such as temperature, humidity, and vibrations to reduce their impact on precision. Use vibration-free tables and enclosures to minimize external influences.
   - ◦ **Stable Conditions**: Conduct measurements in a stable environment where fluctuations in external conditions are minimized.

4. **Proper Instrument Use**:

   - **Follow Manufacturer Guidelines**: Use instruments according to the manufacturer's guidelines to ensure optimal performance. Incorrect use can introduce variability in measurements.
   - **Regular Checks**: Perform regular checks and calibrations to ensure instruments are working correctly and consistently.

5. **Quality Assurance Programs**:

   - **Implement QA/QC Programs**: Establish quality assurance and quality control programs to monitor and improve precision. This includes routine checks, control charts, and internal audits.
   - **Documentation and Review**: Maintain detailed records of all measurements and procedures. Regularly review documentation to identify and address any sources of variability.

Examples of Improving Accuracy and Precision in Common Analytical Procedures:

- **Titration**:

  - **Accuracy**: Standardize titrant solutions regularly against primary standards. Use accurate pipettes and volumetric flasks for sample preparation.
  - **Precision**: Perform titrations in a controlled environment to minimize temperature fluctuations. Use consistent titration techniques and endpoints to ensure reproducibility.

- **Spectroscopy**:

  - **Accuracy**: Calibrate spectrophotometers using standard solutions with known concentrations. Correct for baseline drift and stray light.
  - **Precision**: Perform multiple readings of the same sample and average the results. Ensure that cuvettes are clean and positioned consistently in the instrument.

- **Chromatography**:

- ◦ **Accuracy**: Use certified reference materials to calibrate the chromatographic system. Validate the method for accuracy using recovery studies.
- ◦ **Precision**: Maintain consistent flow rates, injection volumes, and temperature settings. Use replicate injections of the same sample to assess precision.

Example of Implementing Improvements for HPLC Analysis:

1. **Calibration:**

   - ◦ Calibrate the HPLC system using standard solutions of known concentrations. Perform calibration curves and check for linearity across the expected concentration range.

2. **Standard Operating Procedures:**

   - ◦ Develop and follow detailed SOPs for sample preparation, instrument setup, and data analysis. Ensure all analysts are trained to follow these procedures.

3. **Environmental Control:**

   - ◦ Conduct HPLC analyses in a temperature-controlled room to maintain consistent column temperature and minimize variability in retention times.

4. **Replicate Injections:**

   - ◦ Perform replicate injections of each sample to assess the precision of the method. Calculate the relative standard deviation (RSD) to quantify precision.

5. **Quality Control Samples:**

   - ◦ Include quality control samples in each batch of analyses to monitor the accuracy and precision of the HPLC method. Use control charts to track performance over time.

FOUR

PHARMACOPOEIAS AND IMPURITIES

4.1 Overview of Pharmacopoeias

4.1.1 Major Pharmacopoeias (USP, BP, IP, etc.)

Pharmacopoeias are official publications containing a list of medicinal drugs with their effects and directions for their use. They are essential references for ensuring the quality, safety, and efficacy of pharmaceutical products. Pharmacopoeias provide standardized specifications for the identity, purity, and strength of drugs, which are crucial for regulatory compliance and quality control in the pharmaceutical industry. Several major pharmacopoeias are recognized internationally, including the United States Pharmacopoeia (USP), British Pharmacopoeia (BP), and Indian Pharmacopoeia (IP).

United States Pharmacopoeia (USP):

- **History and Purpose**: The USP was first published in 1820 and is a scientific, non-profit organization that sets standards for the quality, purity, strength, and consistency of medicines, food ingredients, and dietary supplements. These standards are recognized and used worldwide.
- **Content**: The USP includes monographs for drug substances, dosage forms, and compounded preparations, providing detailed information on tests, assays, and acceptance criteria. It also covers excipients, dietary supplements, and medical devices.
- **Standards**: The USP standards are legally recognized in the United States and used in over 140 countries. The standards are enforced by the U.S.

Food and Drug Administration (FDA) for drugs marketed in the United States.

- **Updates**: The USP is updated regularly through the USP-NF (United States Pharmacopeia-National Formulary) with new monographs, revisions, and deletions.

British Pharmacopoeia (BP):

- **History and Purpose**: The BP was first published in 1864 and is an official collection of standards for UK medicinal products and pharmaceutical substances. It ensures that medicines are of high quality and are safe for use.
- **Content**: The BP contains monographs for drug substances, formulated preparations, blood products, immunological products, radiopharmaceutical preparations, and surgical materials. Each monograph provides details on the identification, purity tests, assay methods, and storage conditions.
- **Standards**: The BP standards are legally binding in the United Kingdom and are used as reference standards in many other countries. They are recognized by regulatory authorities to ensure the quality of medicinal products.
- **Updates**: The BP is updated annually, with supplementary updates released periodically to incorporate new information and standards.

Indian Pharmacopoeia (IP):

- **History and Purpose**: The IP was first published in 1955 and is the official book of standards for drugs manufactured and marketed in India. It aims to ensure the quality, purity, and strength of medicines available in the Indian market.
- **Content**: The IP includes monographs for drug substances, dosage forms, pharmaceutical aids, and veterinary drugs. It provides specifications for identity, purity, strength, and other quality parameters.
- **Standards**: The IP standards are legally recognized in India and are enforced by the Drug Controller General of India (DCGI) under the Ministry of Health and Family Welfare.
- **Updates**: The IP is updated periodically, with new editions and addenda published to include new monographs and revisions of existing ones.

Other Major Pharmacopoeias:

- **European Pharmacopoeia (Ph. Eur.)**: Published by the European Directorate for the Quality of Medicines & HealthCare (EDQM), it provides common quality standards for medicines in Europe. It includes monographs for active substances, excipients, and dosage forms.
- **Japanese Pharmacopoeia (JP)**: The official standard for medicines in Japan, published by the Japanese Ministry of Health, Labour and Welfare. It includes specifications for the quality and purity of drugs.
- **International Pharmacopoeia (Int. Ph.)**: Published by the World Health Organization (WHO), it aims to provide international standards for pharmaceuticals to promote their quality and consistency worldwide.

Comparison and Harmonization:

- While each pharmacopoeia has its own specific standards and monographs, there is an ongoing effort towards harmonization. Organizations such as the International Council for Harmonisation (ICH) work to align the requirements of different pharmacopoeias to facilitate global trade and regulatory processes.
- Harmonization efforts focus on creating unified standards for pharmaceutical products, reducing redundancy, and ensuring that medicines meet consistent quality standards globally.

Application in Pharmaceutical Industry:

- **Regulatory Compliance**: Pharmaceutical companies must adhere to the standards set by the relevant pharmacopoeia to ensure their products are legally marketable.
- **Quality Control**: Pharmacopoeial standards are used as benchmarks in quality control laboratories to verify the identity, strength, purity, and quality of pharmaceutical products.
- **Research and Development**: Pharmacopoeias provide essential guidelines for the development of new drugs, ensuring that they meet the required quality standards from the outset.

4.1.2 Role and Importance

Pharmacopoeias play a crucial role in the pharmaceutical industry by providing standardized guidelines and specifications for the quality, safety, and efficacy of medicinal products. These official publications serve as authoritative references for manufacturers, regulatory authorities, healthcare professionals, and researchers. The role and importance of pharmacopoeias can be understood through various key aspects:

Ensuring Drug Quality:

- **Standardized Specifications**: Pharmacopoeias provide detailed monographs that outline the specific criteria for the identity, purity, strength, and composition of drugs and their formulations. These specifications ensure that all batches of a product meet the same quality standards, reducing variability and ensuring consistency.
- **Quality Control**: Laboratories use pharmacopoeial standards to perform quality control tests on raw materials, intermediates, and finished products. This helps in identifying any deviations from the accepted standards, allowing for corrective actions to be taken before the product reaches the market.

Protecting Public Health:

- **Safety and Efficacy**: By setting stringent quality standards, pharmacopoeias help ensure that medicinal products are safe for consumption and effective in treating the conditions for which they are prescribed. This is vital for maintaining public trust in pharmaceutical products.
- **Adverse Effects Monitoring**: Pharmacopoeias include guidelines for detecting and quantifying impurities and contaminants that could potentially harm patients. Regular updates incorporate new findings and standards to address emerging safety concerns.

Regulatory Compliance:

- **Legal Framework**: Pharmacopoeial standards are often legally binding, and compliance with these standards is required for the approval and marketing of pharmaceutical products. Regulatory authorities, such as the FDA in the United States, MHRA in the United Kingdom, and CDSCO in India, enforce these standards to ensure that only high-quality products are available to the public.

- **International Trade**: Compliance with pharmacopoeial standards facilitates international trade of pharmaceutical products by ensuring that they meet the quality requirements of different countries. Harmonization efforts among major pharmacopoeias help streamline the regulatory approval process across different regions.

Facilitating Research and Development:

- **Guidelines for New Drugs**: Pharmacopoeias provide essential guidelines and methodologies for the development of new drugs. Researchers and developers use these standards to design robust and reproducible experiments, ensuring that new products meet the required quality criteria from the early stages of development.
- **Innovative Methods**: Pharmacopoeias continuously update their content to include new analytical methods, technologies, and scientific advancements. This encourages innovation and the adoption of best practices in pharmaceutical research and development.

Supporting Healthcare Professionals:

- **Reference for Formulary**: Pharmacopoeias serve as comprehensive references for healthcare professionals, including pharmacists and physicians, who need reliable information about the drugs they prescribe and dispense. This includes details on dosage forms, administration routes, and potential interactions.
- **Education and Training**: Pharmacopoeias are valuable educational tools for training future pharmacists, chemists, and healthcare professionals. They provide a standardized body of knowledge that is essential for understanding drug quality and safety.

Example of Pharmacopoeial Impact:

- **Quality Control Example**: A pharmaceutical company producing a generic drug must adhere to the standards set by the USP for that particular medication. The company's quality control lab tests each batch of the drug against the monograph specifications, including assays for active ingredients, identification tests, and impurity profiles. By meeting these standards, the company ensures that its product is safe, effective, and compliant with regulatory requirements.

- **Regulatory Compliance Example**: Before a new drug can be marketed in multiple countries, it must meet the standards of the relevant pharmacopoeias (e.g., USP, BP, and IP). Harmonized standards help streamline the approval process, enabling the drug to be quickly approved and distributed in different regions, thus ensuring timely access to new therapies for patients worldwide.

Global Harmonization and Collaboration:

- **Harmonization Efforts**: Organizations like the International Council for Harmonisation (ICH) work towards harmonizing pharmacopoeial standards across different regions. This reduces redundancy, simplifies regulatory submissions, and ensures that drugs meet consistent quality standards globally.
- **Collaboration Among Pharmacopoeias**: Major pharmacopoeias such as USP, BP, and IP collaborate to share scientific information and harmonize methods and specifications. This collaboration enhances the global quality of medicines and facilitates international trade and regulatory processes.

4.2 Sources of Impurities
4.2.1 Raw Materials

Raw materials used in the manufacturing of pharmaceutical products are a primary source of impurities. These impurities can arise from various stages of the raw material lifecycle, including sourcing, processing, and handling. Understanding the sources of these impurities is crucial for ensuring the quality and safety of the final pharmaceutical product. Here, we will discuss the types of impurities that can originate from raw materials, their potential sources, and methods to control and minimize them.

Types of Impurities in Raw Materials:

1. **Organic Impurities**: These can include starting materials, by-products, intermediates, degradation products, and reagents used in synthesis.
2. **Inorganic Impurities**: These typically consist of residual metals, reagents, ligands, catalysts, inorganic salts, and other chemicals used in

the manufacturing process.

3. **Residual Solvents**: Organic solvents used in the manufacturing process that are not completely removed during purification.
4. **Microbial Contaminants**: Bacteria, fungi, or viruses that may contaminate raw materials during handling and storage.

Potential Sources of Impurities in Raw Materials:

1. **Sourcing and Quality of Raw Materials**:

   - **Supplier Variability**: Different suppliers may provide raw materials with varying levels of purity and different impurity profiles. The source and geographical origin of raw materials can also affect their quality.
   - **Contaminated Sources**: Raw materials sourced from contaminated environments, such as polluted water or soil, can introduce impurities.
   - **Batch-to-Batch Variability**: Variations between batches from the same supplier can occur due to differences in production methods, raw material sourcing, or environmental conditions.

2. **Manufacturing Processes**:

   - **Chemical Synthesis**: Impurities can form during chemical synthesis due to incomplete reactions, side reactions, or degradation of intermediates.
   - **Purification Processes**: Inadequate purification methods can fail to remove impurities effectively. For example, insufficient washing or filtration can leave residual contaminants.
   - **Storage Conditions**: Improper storage of raw materials, such as exposure to moisture, light, or air, can lead to degradation and the formation of impurities.

3. **Handling and Transport**:

   - **Cross-Contamination**: Raw materials can be contaminated during handling and transport if proper precautions are not taken. For instance, using contaminated containers or equipment can introduce impurities.

- **Environmental Exposure**: Exposure to environmental contaminants such as dust, aerosols, or other chemicals during transport and handling can lead to contamination.

4. **Microbial Contamination**:

- **Natural Sources**: Raw materials derived from natural sources (e.g., plant extracts) are more susceptible to microbial contamination.
- **Improper Handling**: Inadequate handling practices, such as not following aseptic techniques, can introduce microbial contaminants.

Control and Minimization of Impurities in Raw Materials:

1. **Supplier Qualification and Audits**:

- **Supplier Qualification**: Select suppliers based on their ability to provide high-quality raw materials consistently. Perform thorough evaluations of suppliers' manufacturing processes, quality control measures, and impurity profiles.
- **Regular Audits**: Conduct regular audits of suppliers to ensure compliance with quality standards and identify any potential sources of impurities.

2. **Quality Control Testing**:

- **Incoming Material Testing**: Implement rigorous testing of raw materials upon receipt to identify and quantify impurities. Tests should include assays for organic and inorganic impurities, residual solvents, and microbial contaminants.
- **Certificate of Analysis (CoA)**: Require suppliers to provide a CoA for each batch of raw material, detailing the results of impurity testing.

3. **Stringent Storage and Handling Practices**:

- **Proper Storage Conditions**: Store raw materials under conditions that prevent contamination and degradation, such as controlled temperature, humidity, and light exposure.

- **Handling Procedures**: Implement and enforce strict handling procedures to prevent cross-contamination. Use dedicated equipment and facilities for different materials where necessary.

4. **Advanced Purification Techniques**:

   - **Filtration and Washing**: Use advanced filtration and washing techniques to remove impurities effectively. Multiple purification steps may be necessary for materials with high impurity levels.
   - **Chromatography and Crystallization**: Employ techniques such as chromatography and crystallization to achieve higher purity levels by separating impurities from the desired product.

5. **Process Optimization**:

   - **Reaction Conditions**: Optimize reaction conditions in chemical synthesis to minimize the formation of by-products and incomplete reactions.
   - **Purification Protocols**: Develop robust purification protocols tailored to the specific impurity profiles of raw materials.

Example of Controlling Impurities in Raw Materials:

- **Herbal Extracts**: Herbal extracts are susceptible to both organic and microbial impurities. To control these, the following steps can be taken:

  - **Supplier Qualification**: Select suppliers with good agricultural and collection practices (GACP) certification.
  - **Quality Control**: Perform microbial testing and assay for organic impurities using techniques like HPLC and GC-MS.
  - **Storage**: Store extracts in airtight containers away from light and moisture.
  - **Handling**: Use aseptic techniques during handling and processing to prevent microbial contamination.

4.2 Sources of Impurities
4.2.2 Manufacturing Process

The **manufacturing process** of pharmaceutical products is a critical source of impurities. These impurities can arise at various stages of production, including synthesis, formulation, and packaging. Identifying and controlling these impurities is essential for ensuring the quality, safety, and efficacy of the final product.

Types of Impurities in the Manufacturing Process:

1. **Organic Impurities**: These include starting materials, by-products, intermediates, degradation products, and residual solvents used in the manufacturing process.
2. **Inorganic Impurities**: These consist of residual metals, reagents, ligands, catalysts, and other inorganic compounds introduced during synthesis.
3. **Process-Related Contaminants**: These include contaminants introduced through equipment, packaging materials, or environmental sources during the manufacturing process.
4. **Microbial Contaminants**: These are bacteria, fungi, or viruses that may contaminate the product during various stages of manufacturing.

Potential Sources of Impurities in the Manufacturing Process:

1. **Chemical Synthesis:**

   - **Incomplete Reactions**: Incomplete reactions can lead to the presence of unreacted starting materials and intermediates in the final product.
   - **Side Reactions**: Unintended side reactions can produce unwanted by-products that contaminate the final product.
   - **Residual Solvents**: Organic solvents used in synthesis may not be completely removed during purification, leaving residual solvents in the product.

2. **Formulation and Mixing:**

   - **Improper Mixing**: Inadequate mixing of raw materials can result in uneven distribution of active ingredients and excipients, leading to variability and impurities.
   - **Contaminated Excipients**: Excipients used in formulation can introduce impurities if they are not of pharmaceutical grade or

properly tested.

3. **Purification Processes**:

   - **Inefficient Purification**: Insufficient purification methods may fail to remove impurities completely, leaving residual contaminants in the product.
   - **Degradation During Purification**: Harsh purification conditions can cause degradation of the product, leading to the formation of degradation products.

4. **Equipment and Facility Contaminants**:

   - **Cross-Contamination**: Cross-contamination can occur if the same equipment is used for multiple products without proper cleaning. Residues from previous batches can contaminate subsequent products.
   - **Leachables and Extractables**: Materials used in equipment, containers, and packaging can leach chemicals into the product, introducing impurities.

5. **Environmental Contaminants**:

   - **Airborne Particles**: Dust, particulate matter, and aerosols in the manufacturing environment can contaminate the product.
   - **Microbial Contamination**: Poor aseptic techniques, inadequate sterilization, and unclean facilities can lead to microbial contamination.

Control and Minimization of Impurities in the Manufacturing Process:

1. **Process Validation and Optimization**:

   - **Validate Manufacturing Processes**: Thoroughly validate manufacturing processes to ensure they consistently produce products of the desired quality. Validation should include identifying critical process parameters and establishing control limits.

- **Optimize Reaction Conditions**: Optimize reaction conditions to minimize side reactions and maximize the yield of the desired product. This includes controlling temperature, pressure, pH, and reaction time.

2. **Advanced Purification Techniques**:

   - **Use of High-Performance Purification Methods**: Employ advanced purification techniques such as high-performance liquid chromatography (HPLC), recrystallization, and distillation to remove impurities effectively.
   - **Multiple Purification Steps**: Implement multiple purification steps if necessary to achieve the required purity levels.

3. **Quality Control Testing**:

   - **Routine Testing for Impurities**: Conduct routine testing for impurities at various stages of the manufacturing process. This includes testing for organic and inorganic impurities, residual solvents, and microbial contaminants.
   - **In-Process Controls**: Establish in-process controls to monitor critical parameters and detect impurities early in the manufacturing process.

4. **Proper Equipment Maintenance and Cleaning**:

   - **Regular Maintenance**: Perform regular maintenance and calibration of equipment to ensure they function correctly and do not introduce contaminants.
   - **Cleaning Validation**: Implement rigorous cleaning validation procedures to prevent cross-contamination between batches. This includes validating cleaning methods and establishing acceptable residue limits.

5. **Environmental Controls**:

   - **Controlled Manufacturing Environment**: Maintain a controlled manufacturing environment with proper air filtration, temperature, and humidity controls to minimize environmental contaminants.

- **Aseptic Techniques**: Follow strict aseptic techniques and sterilization procedures to prevent microbial contamination.

6. **Training and Standard Operating Procedures (SOPs)**:

   - **Comprehensive Training**: Provide comprehensive training for all personnel involved in the manufacturing process to ensure they understand and follow procedures correctly.
   - **Detailed SOPs**: Develop and adhere to detailed SOPs for every stage of the manufacturing process, including synthesis, formulation, purification, and packaging.

Example of Controlling Impurities in the Manufacturing Process:

- **API Production**: In the production of active pharmaceutical ingredients (APIs), the following steps can be taken to control impurities:

  - **Optimized Synthesis**: Develop optimized synthetic routes to reduce by-products and improve yield. Use catalysts and reagents that minimize side reactions.
  - **Purification**: Employ multiple purification techniques, such as crystallization followed by HPLC, to achieve high purity levels.
  - **Residual Solvent Removal**: Use techniques such as rotary evaporation and vacuum drying to remove residual solvents effectively.
  - **In-Process Monitoring**: Implement in-process monitoring to check for impurities at critical stages. For example, use gas chromatography (GC) to monitor residual solvents.

4.2 Sources of Impurities

4.2.3 Storage Conditions

Storage conditions play a critical role in maintaining the quality and purity of pharmaceutical products. Improper storage can lead to the introduction or increase of impurities through degradation, contamination, or chemical interactions. Understanding the sources of impurities related to storage conditions and implementing proper storage practices are essential for ensuring the stability and efficacy of pharmaceutical products.

Types of Impurities Related to Storage Conditions:

1. **Degradation Products**: Chemical or physical degradation of active pharmaceutical ingredients (APIs) and excipients can result in the formation of impurities.
2. **Contaminants**: External contaminants, such as dust, moisture, and microorganisms, can be introduced during storage.
3. **Interactions with Packaging Materials**: Chemical interactions between the product and its packaging materials can lead to the formation of impurities.

Potential Sources of Impurities Due to Storage Conditions:

1. **Temperature Variations**:

   - **Heat-Induced Degradation**: Elevated temperatures can accelerate chemical reactions, leading to the degradation of APIs and excipients. For example, heat can cause hydrolysis, oxidation, or other decomposition reactions.
   - **Freezing**: Freezing can cause crystallization or phase separation in liquid formulations, leading to instability and degradation.

2. **Humidity and Moisture**:

   - **Hydrolysis**: Exposure to high humidity can result in the hydrolysis of susceptible compounds, forming degradation products.
   - **Microbial Growth**: Moist environments can promote microbial growth, leading to contamination of the product.

3. **Light Exposure**:

   - **Photodegradation**: Exposure to light, especially UV light, can cause photodegradation of light-sensitive compounds, resulting in the formation of impurities.

4. **Air and Oxygen Exposure**:

   - **Oxidation**: Oxygen in the air can oxidize sensitive compounds, leading to the formation of oxidative degradation products.

5. **Packaging Materials**:

- **Leachables and Extractables**: Chemicals from packaging materials can leach into the product, introducing impurities. This is particularly common with plastic containers and rubber stoppers.
- **Interactions**: Chemical interactions between the product and packaging materials can lead to degradation.

Control and Minimization of Impurities Due to Storage Conditions:

1. **Temperature Control**:

- **Controlled Storage Conditions**: Store products at recommended temperatures to prevent heat-induced degradation. Use temperature-controlled storage areas such as refrigerators or climate-controlled rooms.
- **Temperature Monitoring**: Implement continuous temperature monitoring to ensure storage conditions remain within specified limits. Use alarms to alert when temperatures deviate from acceptable ranges.

2. **Humidity Control**:

- **Desiccants**: Use desiccants in packaging to absorb moisture and maintain low humidity levels. Silica gel packets or molecular sieves can be effective.
- **Humidity-Controlled Storage**: Store products in humidity-controlled environments, especially for hygroscopic materials. Use dehumidifiers or humidity-controlled cabinets.

3. **Light Protection**:

- **Opaque Packaging**: Use opaque or amber-colored containers to protect light-sensitive products from photodegradation.
- **Dark Storage Areas**: Store products in dark areas or away from direct light sources. Use light-proof storage units if necessary.

4. **Oxygen Control**:

- ○ **Inert Atmosphere**: Store sensitive products in an inert atmosphere, such as nitrogen or argon, to prevent oxidation. This can be done using sealed containers with inert gas flushing.
- ○ **Oxygen Absorbers**: Include oxygen absorbers in packaging to reduce the oxygen content and prevent oxidation.

5. **Packaging Materials**:

- ○ **Compatibility Testing**: Conduct compatibility testing between the product and packaging materials to identify potential interactions. Select packaging materials that do not react with or leach into the product.
- ○ **Barrier Packaging**: Use barrier packaging materials, such as foil laminates, to protect the product from environmental factors like moisture and oxygen.

6. **Proper Handling and Storage Practices**:

- ○ **Clean Storage Areas**: Maintain clean and sanitary storage areas to prevent contamination from dust, microorganisms, and other contaminants.
- ○ **Proper Labeling**: Clearly label storage areas and containers with temperature, humidity, and light exposure requirements to ensure proper handling.

Example of Implementing Proper Storage Conditions:

1. **Storage of Temperature-Sensitive Drugs**:

- ○ **Controlled Temperature Storage**: Store vaccines and biologics in refrigerators at 2-8°C. Use continuous temperature monitoring systems to ensure the temperature remains within the required range.
- ○ **Temperature-Excursion Protocols**: Develop protocols for handling temperature excursions, including immediate actions and documentation.

2. **Storage of Hygroscopic Powders**:

- **Use of Desiccants**: Include silica gel packets in the packaging of hygroscopic powders to absorb moisture.
- **Humidity-Controlled Rooms**: Store the powders in humidity-controlled rooms maintained at low humidity levels (below 30% RH).

3. **Storage of Light-Sensitive Compounds**:

- **Opaque Containers**: Package light-sensitive compounds in amber glass bottles or opaque plastic containers.
- **Dark Storage**: Store these containers in dark cabinets or rooms to minimize light exposure.

4. **Storage of Oxygen-Sensitive Products**:

- **Inert Gas Flushing**: Store oxygen-sensitive products in sealed containers flushed with nitrogen to displace oxygen.
- **Oxygen Absorbers**: Include oxygen absorber packets in the packaging to further reduce oxygen levels.

4.2 Sources of Impurities
4.2.4 Types of Impurities

In pharmaceutical products, **impurities** can arise from various sources and can be classified based on their origin and nature. Understanding the types of impurities is crucial for their identification, quantification, and control to ensure the quality, safety, and efficacy of pharmaceutical products.

1. Organic Impurities: Organic impurities are chemical compounds that are not the active pharmaceutical ingredient (API) and can include by-products, intermediates, degradation products, and residual solvents. These impurities can originate from the synthesis, storage, or degradation of the API or excipients.

- **Starting Materials and Intermediates**: Impurities can include unreacted starting materials or intermediates used in the synthesis of the API.

  - **Example**: If benzene is used as a starting material in the synthesis of an API, traces of benzene might be present as an impurity in the final product.

- **By-products**: Unintended chemical reactions during synthesis can produce by-products that remain in the final product.

  - **Example**: During the synthesis of a drug, side reactions might produce structurally related compounds that are present as impurities.

- **Degradation Products**: APIs and excipients can degrade over time or under adverse conditions, forming impurities.

  - **Example**: Aspirin can hydrolyze to form salicylic acid and acetic acid, which are considered degradation impurities.

- **Residual Solvents**: Solvents used during synthesis, purification, or formulation that are not completely removed can remain as impurities.

  - **Example**: Residual amounts of methanol or dichloromethane used in the manufacturing process.

2. Inorganic Impurities: Inorganic impurities typically include metals, inorganic salts, and other inorganic substances that can originate from reagents, catalysts, or equipment used during the manufacturing process.

- **Residual Metals**: Metals from catalysts or metal-based reagents can remain in the final product.

  - **Example**: Palladium residues from catalytic hydrogenation processes.

- **Reagents and Salts**: Inorganic reagents or by-products from synthesis can be present as impurities.

  - **Example**: Sodium chloride or sulfuric acid residues from reaction processes.

- **Contaminants from Equipment**: Particles or residues from manufacturing equipment or containers.

  - **Example**: Iron particles from equipment corrosion.

3. Residual Solvents: These are organic volatile chemicals used or produced during the manufacturing process. Their presence is controlled because they can have toxic effects and impact the quality of the product.

- **Class 1 Solvents**: Solvents to be avoided due to their known human carcinogenicity or environmental hazards.

  - **Example**: Benzene, carbon tetrachloride.

- **Class 2 Solvents**: Solvents to be limited due to their inherent toxicity.

  - **Example**: Methanol, toluene.

- **Class 3 Solvents**: Solvents with low toxic potential that should be used and controlled appropriately.

  - **Example**: Ethanol, acetone.

4. Microbial Contaminants: Microbial contamination can arise from the environment, raw materials, or during the manufacturing process, affecting the product's safety and efficacy.

- **Bacteria**: Pathogenic and non-pathogenic bacteria can contaminate pharmaceutical products.

  - **Example**: Escherichia coli, Staphylococcus aureus.

- **Fungi and Molds**: Spores and mycelia can contaminate products, particularly in humid conditions.

  - **Example**: Aspergillus niger, Candida albicans.

- **Endotoxins**: Toxins from Gram-negative bacteria that can cause severe reactions.

  - **Example**: Lipopolysaccharides from E. coli.

5. Other Impurities: These impurities can be from miscellaneous sources and might include contaminants from the environment, packaging materials, or storage conditions.

- **Leachables and Extractables**: Chemicals that leach out from packaging materials or are extracted during contact with the product.

  - **Example**: Phthalates from plastic containers, antioxidants from rubber stoppers.

- **Environmental Contaminants**: Dust, particulate matter, or other contaminants introduced during manufacturing or storage.

  - **Example**: Dust particles, fibers.

Control and Minimization of Impurities:

1. **Quality Control Testing**:

   - Conduct routine testing for organic and inorganic impurities, residual solvents, and microbial contaminants using validated analytical methods.
   - Implement strict acceptance criteria and ensure compliance with regulatory standards such as ICH guidelines.

2. **Process Optimization**:

   - Optimize synthesis routes to minimize the formation of by-products and residual starting materials.
   - Use high-purity reagents and solvents to reduce the introduction of impurities.

3. **Purification Techniques**:

   - Employ advanced purification techniques such as crystallization, distillation, and chromatography to remove impurities.
   - Ensure adequate washing and drying processes to eliminate residual solvents and reagents.

4. **Proper Storage and Handling**:

   - Store raw materials and finished products under controlled conditions to prevent degradation and contamination.
   - Use appropriate packaging materials to minimize leachables and protect against environmental contaminants.

5. **Environmental Control**:

   - Maintain clean and controlled manufacturing environments to reduce the risk of microbial contamination.
   - Implement aseptic techniques and use sterilization procedures where necessary.

6. **Regular Audits and Supplier Qualification**:

   - Conduct regular audits of suppliers to ensure they comply with quality standards and do not introduce impurities.
   - Qualify and monitor suppliers to ensure the consistency and purity of raw materials.

Example of Impurity Control in a Pharmaceutical Product:

- **Drug Substance**: During the synthesis of a drug substance, ensure that the reaction conditions are optimized to minimize by-products. Use high-purity starting materials and reagents.
- **Purification**: Use chromatography to separate the desired product from impurities. Employ crystallization to further purify the drug substance.
- **Storage**: Store the purified drug substance in airtight containers under nitrogen to prevent oxidation and moisture uptake.
- **Quality Control**: Perform HPLC and GC analysis to detect and quantify organic impurities and residual solvents. Conduct metal analysis using ICP-MS to detect residual metals.

4.3 Limit Tests
4.3.1 Purpose and Procedures

Limit tests are qualitative or semi-quantitative tests used in the pharmaceutical industry to ensure that the levels of specific impurities in drug substances or products do not exceed established limits. These tests are crucial for maintaining the safety, efficacy, and quality of pharmaceutical products. The primary purpose of limit tests is to detect and control impurities that can affect the drug's performance or pose a risk to patient health.

Purpose of Limit Tests:

1. **Safety**: Ensuring that toxic impurities, such as heavy metals or harmful chemicals, are present only at permissible levels to avoid adverse effects on patients.
2. **Quality Control**: Verifying that pharmaceutical products meet the stringent quality standards required by regulatory agencies.
3. **Regulatory Compliance**: Complying with pharmacopeial standards and regulatory requirements, such as those set by the USP, BP, IP, and other international guidelines.
4. **Consistency**: Maintaining batch-to-batch consistency in the quality of pharmaceutical products by controlling impurity levels.

Common Impurities Tested in Limit Tests:

- Heavy metals (e.g., lead, mercury, cadmium)
- Chlorides
- Sulfates
- Iron
- Arsenic

Procedures for Common Limit Tests:

1. **Limit Test for Chlorides**:

   - **Purpose**: To ensure that the chloride content in a sample does not exceed the specified limit.
   - **Procedure**:

     1. **Preparation of Sample Solution**: Dissolve a specified amount of the sample in water and transfer to a Nessler cylinder.
     2. **Addition of Reagents**: Add a few drops of nitric acid and silver nitrate solution to the sample solution.

3. **Observation**: Compare the turbidity of the sample solution to that of a standard solution containing a known concentration of chloride.
4. **Interpretation**: If the turbidity of the sample solution is less than or equal to the standard solution, the sample passes the test for chlorides.

2. **Limit Test for Sulfates**:

- **Purpose**: To ensure that the sulfate content in a sample does not exceed the specified limit.
- **Procedure**:

   1. **Preparation of Sample Solution**: Dissolve a specified amount of the sample in water and transfer to a Nessler cylinder.
   2. **Addition of Reagents**: Add barium chloride solution and hydrochloric acid to the sample solution.
   3. **Observation**: Compare the turbidity of the sample solution to that of a standard solution containing a known concentration of sulfate.
   4. **Interpretation**: If the turbidity of the sample solution is less than or equal to the standard solution, the sample passes the test for sulfates.

3. **Limit Test for Heavy Metals**:

- **Purpose**: To ensure that the total heavy metal content in a sample does not exceed the specified limit.
- **Procedure**:

   1. **Preparation of Sample Solution**: Digest a specified amount of the sample with nitric acid and hydrochloric acid.
   2. **Addition of Reagents**: Add ammonium citrate, hydroxylamine hydrochloride, and a dithizone solution to the sample solution.
   3. **Extraction**: Extract the colored complex formed with chloroform and compare the color intensity with a standard solution.
   4. **Interpretation**: If the color intensity of the sample solution is less than or equal to the standard solution, the sample passes the test

for heavy metals.

4. **Limit Test for Iron**:

   - **Purpose**: To ensure that the iron content in a sample does not exceed the specified limit.
   - **Procedure**:

     1. **Preparation of Sample Solution**: Dissolve a specified amount of the sample in hydrochloric acid and transfer to a Nessler cylinder.
     2. **Addition of Reagents**: Add ammonium thiocyanate solution to the sample solution.
     3. **Observation**: Compare the red color intensity of the sample solution to that of a standard solution containing a known concentration of iron.
     4. **Interpretation**: If the red color intensity of the sample solution is less than or equal to the standard solution, the sample passes the test for iron.

5. **Limit Test for Arsenic**:

   - **Purpose**: To ensure that the arsenic content in a sample does not exceed the specified limit.
   - **Procedure**:

     1. **Preparation of Sample Solution**: Mix the sample with hydrochloric acid and transfer to a suitable apparatus for arsenic detection.
     2. **Addition of Reagents**: Add zinc and potassium iodide to generate arsine gas.
     3. **Detection**: Pass the arsine gas through a paper impregnated with mercuric chloride.
     4. **Observation**: Compare the stain on the paper with a standard stain produced by a known amount of arsenic.
     5. **Interpretation**: If the stain from the sample is lighter than or matches the standard stain, the sample passes the test for arsenic.

General Considerations for Limit Tests:

- **Reagent Quality**: Use high-purity reagents and standard solutions to ensure the accuracy of the test.
- **Glassware**: Clean glassware thoroughly to avoid contamination that could affect the results.
- **Standard Solutions**: Prepare standard solutions with precision, using accurately weighed and dissolved reference materials.
- **Environmental Control**: Conduct tests in a controlled environment to minimize interference from external factors such as dust or humidity.

Example of Performing a Limit Test for Heavy Metals:

1. **Sample Preparation**:

   - Weigh 1 gram of the sample and transfer it to a beaker.
   - Add 10 mL of nitric acid and heat gently until the sample is completely digested.
   - Cool the solution and add 10 mL of hydrochloric acid.

2. **Reagent Addition**:

   - Add 2 mL of ammonium citrate solution and mix.
   - Add 1 mL of hydroxylamine hydrochloride solution and mix.
   - Add 2 mL of dithizone solution and shake well.

3. **Extraction**:

   - Transfer the mixture to a separatory funnel and add 10 mL of chloroform.
   - Shake the funnel vigorously and allow the layers to separate.

4. **Observation**:

   - Compare the color intensity of the chloroform layer with that of a standard solution containing a known concentration of heavy metals.

5. **Interpretation**:

- ○ If the color intensity of the chloroform layer is less than or equal to the standard solution, the sample passes the test for heavy metals.

4.3 Limit Tests
4.3.2 Limit Test for Chlorides

Purpose: The limit test for chlorides is designed to ensure that the chloride content in a pharmaceutical substance does not exceed the specified limit. Chloride ions can be present as impurities due to various sources, including raw materials, manufacturing processes, and environmental contamination. This test is crucial for maintaining the quality and safety of pharmaceutical products.

Principle: The test is based on the reaction of chloride ions with silver nitrate in the presence of nitric acid, resulting in the formation of a white precipitate of silver chloride. The turbidity produced is compared to that of a standard solution containing a known concentration of chloride ions.

Reagents and Materials:

- **Nitric Acid (HNO_3)**: Concentrated, to acidify the solution.
- **Silver Nitrate Solution ($AgNO_3$)**: Aqueous solution, which reacts with chloride ions to form a precipitate.
- **Standard Chloride Solution**: A solution with a known concentration of chloride ions, used for comparison.
- **Distilled Water**: To prepare solutions and dilute samples.
- **Nessler Cylinders**: For visual comparison of turbidity.

Procedure:

1. **Preparation of Sample Solution**:

   - ○ Weigh an appropriate amount of the sample, as specified in the monograph, and dissolve it in distilled water.
   - ○ Transfer the solution to a Nessler cylinder and dilute to the required volume, usually 50 mL.

2. **Preparation of Standard Chloride Solution**:

   - ○ Prepare a standard chloride solution by dissolving a known amount of sodium chloride (NaCl) in distilled water to achieve a specific concentration (e.g., 10 ppm Cl⁻).

- Transfer the standard chloride solution to a separate Nessler cylinder and dilute to the same volume as the sample solution (usually 50 mL).

3. **Addition of Nitric Acid**:

- To both the sample solution and the standard chloride solution, add 1 mL of concentrated nitric acid. Mix thoroughly.

4. **Addition of Silver Nitrate**:

- Add 1 mL of silver nitrate solution to both the sample and standard solutions. The addition of silver nitrate should be done carefully to avoid excess precipitation.
- Mix the solutions thoroughly and allow them to stand for five minutes for the precipitate to form and settle.

5. **Comparison**:

- Visually compare the turbidity of the sample solution with that of the standard solution against a dark background.
- Ensure both solutions are viewed under the same lighting conditions for an accurate comparison.

6. **Interpretation**:

- If the turbidity of the sample solution is less than or equal to that of the standard chloride solution, the sample passes the limit test for chlorides.
- If the sample solution is more turbid than the standard, it indicates that the chloride content exceeds the specified limit.

Example:

1. **Sample Preparation**:

- Weigh 1.0 g of the pharmaceutical substance and dissolve it in 50 mL of distilled water in a Nessler cylinder.

2. **Standard Solution Preparation**:

   - Prepare a standard chloride solution by dissolving 0.0824 g of sodium chloride in 1 liter of distilled water (10 ppm Cl^-).
   - Take 50 mL of this standard chloride solution in a separate Nessler cylinder.

3. **Procedure**:

   - Add 1 mL of concentrated nitric acid to each Nessler cylinder and mix well.
   - Add 1 mL of silver nitrate solution to each cylinder and mix thoroughly.
   - Allow the solutions to stand for five minutes.

4. **Comparison**:

   - Compare the turbidity of the sample solution to the standard chloride solution.
   - If the sample solution's turbidity is less than or equal to the standard, the sample passes the test.

Precautions:

- Ensure all glassware and reagents are clean and free from chloride contamination.
- Handle nitric acid and silver nitrate with care, as they are corrosive and can cause skin irritation.
- Perform the test under consistent lighting conditions to ensure accurate visual comparison.

When **chloride ions (Cl^-)** react with **silver nitrate ($AgNO_3$)** in the presence of **nitric acid (HNO_3)**, a white precipitate of **silver chloride (AgCl)** is formed. The reaction is as follows:

$$Cl^- + AgNO_3 \rightarrow AgCl\downarrow + NO_3^-$$

The presence of nitric acid helps to keep the solution acidic and prevents the precipitation of other silver salts, ensuring that only silver chloride precipitates out.

Steps of the Reaction Process:

1. **Addition of Nitric Acid**: $HNO_3 \rightarrow NO_3 + H^+$ Nitric acid dissociates into nitrate ions (NO_3) and hydrogen ions (H^+). The acidic medium helps to dissolve any interfering substances and keeps the chloride ions in solution.
2. **Addition of Silver Nitrate**: $AgNO_3 \rightarrow Ag^+ + NO^{3-}$ Silver nitrate dissociates into silver ions (Ag^+) and nitrate ions (NO^{3-}).
3. **Formation of Silver Chloride Precipitate**: $Ag^+ + Cl- \rightarrow AgCl\downarrow$

Silver ions react with chloride ions to form a white precipitate of silver chloride (AgCl).

4.3 Limit Tests

4.3.3 Limit Test for Sulphates

Purpose: The limit test for sulphates is designed to ensure that the sulphate content in a pharmaceutical substance does not exceed the specified limit. Sulphates can be present as impurities due to various sources such as raw materials, manufacturing processes, and environmental contamination. This test is essential for maintaining the quality and safety of pharmaceutical products.

Principle: The test is based on the reaction of sulphate ions with barium chloride in the presence of hydrochloric acid, resulting in the formation of a white precipitate of barium sulphate. The turbidity produced is compared to that of a standard solution containing a known concentration of sulphate ions.

Reagents and Materials:

- **Hydrochloric Acid (HCl)**: Concentrated, to acidify the solution.
- **Barium Chloride Solution ($BaCl_2$)**: Aqueous solution, which reacts with sulphate ions to form a precipitate.
- **Standard Sulphate Solution**: A solution with a known concentration of sulphate ions, used for comparison.
- **Distilled Water**: To prepare solutions and dilute samples.
- **Nessler Cylinders**: For visual comparison of turbidity.

Procedure:

1. **Preparation of Sample Solution**:

- ○ Weigh an appropriate amount of the sample, as specified in the monograph, and dissolve it in distilled water.
- ○ Transfer the solution to a Nessler cylinder and dilute to the required volume, usually 50 mL.

2. **Preparation of Standard Sulphate Solution:**

- ○ Prepare a standard sulphate solution by dissolving a known amount of potassium sulphate (K_2SO_4) in distilled water to achieve a specific concentration (e.g., 10 ppm SO_4^{2-}).
- ○ Transfer the standard sulphate solution to a separate Nessler cylinder and dilute to the same volume as the sample solution (usually 50 mL).

3. **Addition of Hydrochloric Acid:**

- ○ To both the sample solution and the standard sulphate solution, add 2 mL of concentrated hydrochloric acid. Mix thoroughly. The acidification helps in preventing the precipitation of other salts that might interfere with the test.

4. **Addition of Barium Chloride:**

- ○ Add 1 mL of barium chloride solution to both the sample and standard solutions. The barium chloride reacts with the sulphate ions to form a white precipitate of barium sulphate: $SO_4^{2-} + BaCl_2 \rightarrow BaSO_4 \downarrow + 2Cl$

5. **Observation:**

- ○ Allow the solutions to stand for about 5 minutes for the precipitate to form and settle.
- ○ Visually compare the turbidity of the sample solution with that of the standard solution against a dark background.

6. **Interpretation:**

- ○ If the turbidity of the sample solution is less than or equal to that of the standard solution, the sample passes the limit test for sulphates.

- ○ If the sample solution is more turbid than the standard, it indicates that the sulphate content exceeds the specified limit.

Example:

1. **Sample Preparation:**

   - ○ Weigh 1.0 g of the pharmaceutical substance and dissolve it in 50 mL of distilled water in a Nessler cylinder.

2. **Standard Solution Preparation:**

   - ○ Prepare a standard sulphate solution by dissolving 0.181 g of potassium sulphate in 1 liter of distilled water (10 ppm SO_4^{2-}).
   - ○ Take 50 mL of this standard sulphate solution in a separate Nessler cylinder.

3. **Procedure:**

   - ○ Add 2 mL of concentrated hydrochloric acid to each Nessler cylinder and mix well.
   - ○ Add 1 mL of barium chloride solution to each cylinder and mix thoroughly.
   - ○ Allow the solutions to stand for five minutes.

4. **Comparison:**

   - ○ Compare the turbidity of the sample solution to the standard sulphate solution.
   - ○ If the sample solution's turbidity is less than or equal to the standard, the sample passes the test.

Precautions:

- Ensure all glassware and reagents are clean and free from sulphate contamination.
- Handle hydrochloric acid and barium chloride with care, as they are corrosive and can cause skin irritation.

· Perform the test under consistent lighting conditions to ensure accurate visual comparison.

4.3 Limit Tests
4.3.4 Limit Test for Iron

Purpose: The limit test for iron is designed to ensure that the iron content in a pharmaceutical substance does not exceed the specified limit. Iron can be present as an impurity due to various sources such as raw materials, manufacturing processes, and environmental contamination. This test is crucial for maintaining the quality and safety of pharmaceutical products.

Principle: The test is based on the reaction of iron (III) ions with thioglycolic acid in the presence of citric acid, resulting in the formation of a purple-colored complex. The intensity of the color produced is compared to that of a standard solution containing a known concentration of iron.

Reagents and Materials:

· **Citric Acid Solution**: To complex with iron and prevent interference from other metal ions.
· **Thioglycolic Acid**: To react with iron (III) ions to form a colored complex.
· **Ammonia Solution**: To adjust the pH of the solution.
· **Standard Iron Solution**: A solution with a known concentration of iron, used for comparison.
· **Distilled Water**: To prepare solutions and dilute samples.
· **Nessler Cylinders**: For visual comparison of color intensity.

Procedure:

1. **Preparation of Sample Solution**:

    ○ Weigh an appropriate amount of the sample, as specified in the monograph, and dissolve it in 40 mL of distilled water.
    ○ Transfer the solution to a Nessler cylinder.

2. **Preparation of Standard Iron Solution**:

    ○ Prepare a standard iron solution by dissolving a known amount of iron (III) chloride in distilled water to achieve a specific concentration (e.g., 10 ppm Fe^{3+}).

- Transfer 40 mL of this standard iron solution to a separate Nessler cylinder.

3. **Addition of Citric Acid and Ammonia:**

- To both the sample solution and the standard iron solution, add 2 mL of citric acid solution and 0.1 mL of thioglycolic acid.
- Mix the solutions thoroughly.
- Add dilute ammonia solution dropwise to each cylinder until the solution is just alkaline to litmus paper. Then dilute to 50 mL with distilled water and mix well. The citric acid acts to complex iron and prevent precipitation of other metal ions, and the ammonia adjusts the pH.

4. **Observation:**

- Allow the solutions to stand for about 5 minutes to develop the color.
- Visually compare the color intensity of the sample solution with that of the standard solution against a white background.

5. **Interpretation:**

- If the color intensity of the sample solution is less than or equal to that of the standard solution, the sample passes the limit test for iron.
- If the sample solution is more intense in color than the standard, it indicates that the iron content exceeds the specified limit.

Example:

1. **Sample Preparation:**

- Weigh 1.0 g of the pharmaceutical substance and dissolve it in 40 mL of distilled water in a Nessler cylinder.

2. **Standard Solution Preparation:**

- Prepare a standard iron solution by dissolving 0.1726 g of ferric ammonium sulfate in 1 liter of distilled water (10 ppm Fe^{3+}).
- Take 40 mL of this standard iron solution in a separate Nessler cylinder.

3. **Procedure**:

- Add 2 mL of citric acid solution and 0.1 mL of thioglycolic acid to each Nessler cylinder and mix well.
- Add dilute ammonia solution dropwise until the solution is just alkaline to litmus paper.
- Dilute to 50 mL with distilled water and mix thoroughly.
- Allow the solutions to stand for five minutes.

4. **Comparison**:

- Compare the color intensity of the sample solution to the standard iron solution.
- If the sample solution's color intensity is less than or equal to the standard, the sample passes the test.

Precautions:

- Ensure all glassware and reagents are clean and free from iron contamination.
- Handle thioglycolic acid and ammonia with care, as they are corrosive and can cause skin irritation.
- Perform the test under consistent lighting conditions to ensure accurate visual comparison.

4.3 Limit Tests

4.3.5 Limit Test for Lead

Purpose: The limit test for lead is designed to ensure that the lead content in a pharmaceutical substance does not exceed the specified limit. Lead is a toxic metal that can contaminate pharmaceutical products through raw materials, manufacturing processes, and environmental sources. This test is crucial for maintaining the safety and quality of pharmaceutical products.

Principle: The test is based on the reaction of lead ions with a sulfuric acid-ammonium citrate buffer in the presence of a potassium cyanide solution and a dithizone reagent. Lead forms a complex with dithizone, resulting in a pink to red color, which is compared to a standard lead solution.

Reagents and Materials:

- **Sulfuric Acid-Ammonium Citrate Buffer Solution**: To maintain the pH and prevent precipitation of lead as lead sulfate.
- **Potassium Cyanide Solution**: To complex interfering metals.
- **Dithizone Solution**: An organic reagent that forms a colored complex with lead ions.
- **Standard Lead Solution**: A solution with a known concentration of lead, used for comparison.
- **Distilled Water**: To prepare solutions and dilute samples.
- **Separatory Funnel**: For extraction.
- **Nessler Cylinders**: For visual comparison of color intensity.

Procedure:

1. **Preparation of Sample Solution**:

   - Weigh an appropriate amount of the sample, as specified in the monograph, and dissolve it in distilled water.
   - Transfer the solution to a 50 mL Nessler cylinder.

2. **Preparation of Standard Lead Solution**:

   - Prepare a standard lead solution by dissolving a known amount of lead nitrate in distilled water to achieve a specific concentration (e.g., 10 ppm Pb^{2+}).
   - Transfer 50 mL of this standard lead solution to a separate Nessler cylinder.

3. **Addition of Buffer and Potassium Cyanide**:

   - To both the sample solution and the standard lead solution, add 2 mL of sulfuric acid-ammonium citrate buffer solution. This buffer helps to maintain the pH and prevents the precipitation of lead as lead sulfate.

- Add 1 mL of potassium cyanide solution to each cylinder. Potassium cyanide complexes with interfering metals, preventing them from reacting with dithizone.

4. **Addition of Dithizone Solution:**

- Add 4 mL of dithizone solution to each cylinder and shake vigorously in a separatory funnel for 2 minutes. The dithizone reagent reacts with lead ions to form a colored complex.
- Allow the organic layer to separate from the aqueous layer.

5. **Observation:**

- Transfer the organic (chloroform) layer to a clean Nessler cylinder.
- Visually compare the color intensity of the sample solution with that of the standard solution against a white background.

6. **Interpretation:**

- If the color intensity of the sample solution is less than or equal to that of the standard solution, the sample passes the limit test for lead.
- If the sample solution is more intense in color than the standard, it indicates that the lead content exceeds the specified limit.

Example:

1. **Sample Preparation:**

- Weigh 1.0 g of the pharmaceutical substance and dissolve it in 50 mL of distilled water in a Nessler cylinder.

2. **Standard Solution Preparation:**

- Prepare a standard lead solution by dissolving 0.1598 g of lead nitrate in 1 liter of distilled water (10 ppm Pb^{2+}).

- Take 50 mL of this standard lead solution in a separate Nessler cylinder.

3. **Procedure**:

- Add 2 mL of sulfuric acid-ammonium citrate buffer solution and 1 mL of potassium cyanide solution to each Nessler cylinder and mix well.
- Add 4 mL of dithizone solution to each cylinder and shake vigorously in a separatory funnel for 2 minutes.
- Allow the layers to separate and transfer the organic layer to a clean Nessler cylinder.

4. **Comparison**:

- Compare the color intensity of the sample solution to the standard lead solution.
- If the sample solution's color intensity is less than or equal to the standard, the sample passes the test.

Precautions:

- Ensure all glassware and reagents are clean and free from lead contamination.
- Handle potassium cyanide and dithizone with care, as they are toxic and can cause skin irritation.
- Perform the test under consistent lighting conditions to ensure accurate visual comparison.
- Dispose of all waste, especially cyanide and dithizone solutions, according to safety regulations due to their toxicity.

4.3 Limit Tests
4.3.6 Limit Test for Arsenic
Purpose: The limit test for arsenic is designed to ensure that the arsenic content in a pharmaceutical substance does not exceed the specified limit. Arsenic is a toxic element that can contaminate pharmaceutical products through raw materials, manufacturing processes, and environmental sources. This test is crucial for maintaining the safety and quality of pharmaceutical products.

Principle: The test is based on the generation of arsine gas (AsH_3) from arsenic present in the sample when treated with zinc and acid. The arsine gas is then passed through a paper impregnated with mercuric chloride, which reacts with the gas to form a yellow to brown stain. The intensity of the stain is compared with that produced by a standard arsenic solution.

Reagents and Materials:

- **Hydrochloric Acid (HCl)**: Concentrated, to acidify the solution.
- **Zinc Granules**: To reduce arsenic compounds and generate arsine gas.
- **Stannous Chloride Solution**: To reduce arsenic to its trivalent state.
- **Potassium Iodide Solution**: To enhance the reduction of arsenic.
- **Lead Acetate Cotton**: To absorb any hydrogen sulfide gas produced during the reaction.
- **Mercuric Chloride Paper**: To detect arsine gas.
- **Standard Arsenic Solution**: A solution with a known concentration of arsenic, used for comparison.
- **Distilled Water**: To prepare solutions and dilute samples.
- **Arsenic Apparatus**: A specialized setup to generate and capture arsine gas.

Procedure:

1. **Preparation of Sample Solution**:

   - Weigh an appropriate amount of the sample, as specified in the monograph, and transfer it to the arsenic apparatus.

2. **Preparation of Standard Arsenic Solution**:

   - Prepare a standard arsenic solution by dissolving a known amount of arsenic trioxide in hydrochloric acid and diluting with distilled water to achieve a specific concentration (e.g., 1 ppm As^{3+}).
   - Transfer the standard arsenic solution to a separate arsenic apparatus.

3. **Addition of Reagents**:

- To both the sample solution and the standard arsenic solution, add 5 mL of stannous chloride solution and 5 mL of potassium iodide solution.
- Add 10 mL of hydrochloric acid to each apparatus to acidify the solution.

4. **Generation of Arsine Gas**:

- Add a few zinc granules to each apparatus. The reaction between zinc and hydrochloric acid generates hydrogen gas, which reduces arsenic to arsine gas: $As^{3+}+3Zn+6HCl \rightarrow AsH_3\uparrow+3ZnCl_2+3H_2$

5. **Capture of Arsine Gas**:

- Place a piece of mercuric chloride paper at the top of the apparatus to capture the arsine gas. The reaction between arsine gas and mercuric chloride forms a yellow to brown stain on the paper:
- $AsH_3+3HgCl_2 \rightarrow Hg(AsH_2)_2 + HCl$

6. **Observation**:

- Allow the reaction to proceed for about 40 minutes to ensure complete evolution and absorption of arsine gas.
- Compare the intensity of the stain on the mercuric chloride paper from the sample solution with that from the standard arsenic solution against a white background.

7. **Interpretation**:

- If the intensity of the stain on the sample paper is less than or equal to that of the standard paper, the sample passes the limit test for arsenic.
- If the sample paper shows a more intense stain than the standard, it indicates that the arsenic content exceeds the specified limit.

Example:

1. **Sample Preparation**:

- Weigh 1.0 g of the pharmaceutical substance and transfer it to the arsenic apparatus.

2. **Standard Solution Preparation:**

- Prepare a standard arsenic solution by dissolving 0.00132 g of arsenic trioxide in hydrochloric acid and diluting to 1 liter with distilled water (1 ppm As3+).
- Take 50 mL of this standard arsenic solution in a separate arsenic apparatus.

3. **Procedure:**

- Add 5 mL of stannous chloride solution and 5 mL of potassium iodide solution to each apparatus.
- Add 10 mL of hydrochloric acid to each apparatus and mix well.
- Add a few zinc granules to each apparatus to generate arsine gas.
- Place a piece of mercuric chloride paper at the top of each apparatus to capture the arsine gas.

4. **Observation:**

- Allow the reaction to proceed for 40 minutes.
- Compare the stain intensity on the mercuric chloride paper from the sample solution to the standard arsenic solution.

5. **Comparison:**

- If the stain intensity of the sample solution is less than or equal to the standard, the sample passes the test.

Precautions:

- Ensure all glassware and reagents are clean and free from arsenic contamination.
- Handle hydrochloric acid and mercuric chloride with care, as they are corrosive and toxic.

- Perform the test under consistent lighting conditions to ensure accurate visual comparison.
- Properly dispose of all waste, especially mercuric chloride paper and solutions containing arsenic, according to safety regulations due to their toxicity.

Conclusion: The limit test for arsenic is a sensitive and reliable method for ensuring that pharmaceutical products meet quality standards by controlling the level of arsenic impurities. By following the prescribed procedures and using accurate comparisons, manufacturers can ensure the safety and efficacy of their products.

FIVE

ACID-BASE TITRATIONS

5.1 Theories of Acid-Base Indicators

5.1.1 Acid-Base Indicator Theory

Introduction: Acid-base indicators are substances that change color in response to changes in pH, making them valuable tools in acid-base titrations. These indicators help determine the endpoint of a titration by exhibiting a distinct color change at a particular pH value. The color change is due to the reversible chemical reaction that occurs in the indicator molecule in response to the concentration of hydrogen ions (H^+).

Principle: The theory of acid-base indicators is based on the concept that indicators are weak acids or bases that exhibit different colors in their protonated (HIn) and deprotonated (In^-) forms. The equilibrium between these two forms is pH-dependent, and the color observed is a result of the relative concentrations of the protonated and deprotonated forms.

Chemical Equilibrium: The equilibrium between the protonated and deprotonated forms of an indicator can be represented by the following equation:

$$HIn \rightleftharpoons H^+ + In^-$$

- **HIn**: Protonated form of the indicator (color A).
- **In⁻**: Deprotonated form of the indicator (color B).
- The position of this equilibrium is governed by the concentration of hydrogen ions (H^+), which is related to the pH of the solution.

Henderson-Hasselbalch Equation: The pH at which the indicator changes color can be understood using the Henderson-Hasselbalch equation

$$pH = pKa + \log([In^-]/[HIn])$$

- **pH**: The pH of the solution.
- **pKa**: The acid dissociation constant of the indicator.
- $[In^-]$: Concentration of the deprotonated form.
- **[HIn]**: Concentration of the protonated form.

Color Change Range: The color change of an indicator occurs over a range of pH values, typically within ±1 pH unit of the pKa value of the indicator. Within this range, the indicator transitions from the color of the protonated form to the color of the deprotonated form.

Selection of Indicators: The choice of an appropriate acid-base indicator for a titration depends on the pH range over which the color change occurs and the pH at the equivalence point of the titration. The indicator should have a pKa close to the pH of the equivalence point to ensure a distinct color change at the endpoint.

Examples of Acid-Base Indicators:

1. **Phenolphthalein**:

    - **pH Range**: 8.2 to 10.0
    - **Color Change**: Colorless (HIn) to pink (In^-)
    - **Use**: Suitable for titrations of strong bases against weak acids.

2. **Methyl Orange**:

    - **pH Range**: 3.1 to 4.4
    - **Color Change**: Red (HIn) to yellow (In^-)
    - **Use**: Suitable for titrations of strong acids against weak bases.

3. **Bromothymol Blue**:

    - **pH Range**: 6.0 to 7.6
    - **Color Change**: Yellow (HIn) to blue (In^-)
    - **Use**: Suitable for titrations of strong acids against strong bases.

Mechanism of Color Change:

- The color change in an indicator occurs due to structural changes in the indicator molecule that affect its light absorption properties.
- For instance, in phenolphthalein, the protonated form is colorless because it absorbs light in the ultraviolet region, whereas the deprotonated form is pink because it absorbs light in the visible region.

Detailed Example:
Phenolphthalein:

1. **Chemical Structure**: Phenolphthalein is a weak acid that exists in equilibrium between its colorless protonated form (HIn) and its pink deprotonated form (In⁻).
2. **Equilibrium Reaction**: $HIn \rightleftharpoons H^+ + In^-$
3. **Henderson-Hasselbalch Equation**:

   - At the midpoint of the color change, $[HIn] = [In^-]$, so: $pH = pKa$
   - For phenolphthalein, the pKa is approximately 9.3.

4. **Color Change Range**:

   - Below pH 8.2: The solution remains colorless because the concentration of H^+ is high, favoring the protonated form (HIn).
   - Above pH 10.0: The solution turns pink as the concentration of H^+ decreases, favoring the deprotonated form (In⁻).

5.1 Theories of Acid-Base Indicators
5.1.2 Classification of Indicators

Introduction: Acid-base indicators are compounds that change color at a specific pH range. These indicators are classified based on their chemical nature, the pH range over which they change color, and their application in different types of titrations. Understanding the classification of indicators helps in selecting the appropriate one for a given titration.

Classification Based on Chemical Nature:

1. **Synthetic Indicators**:

   - These are artificially synthesized compounds used to indicate the pH of a solution.

- ○ **Examples**: Phenolphthalein, Methyl Orange, Bromothymol Blue.
- ○ **Use**: Widely used in laboratory titrations due to their well-defined color change properties.

2. **Natural Indicators**:

- ○ These are naturally occurring substances that exhibit a color change in response to pH changes.
- ○ **Examples**: Litmus, Red Cabbage Juice, Turmeric.
- ○ **Use**: Often used in educational demonstrations and simple pH testing.

Classification Based on pH Range of Color Change:

1. **Indicators for Acidic Range (pH < 7)**:

- ○ These indicators change color in acidic conditions.
- ○ **Examples**: Methyl Orange (pH 3.1 to 4.4, red to yellow), Bromophenol Blue (pH 3.0 to 4.6, yellow to blue).
- ○ **Use**: Suitable for titrations involving strong acids and weak bases.

2. **Indicators for Neutral Range (pH ≈ 7)**:

- ○ These indicators exhibit a color change around neutral pH.
- ○ **Examples**: Bromothymol Blue (pH 6.0 to 7.6, yellow to blue), Phenol Red (pH 6.8 to 8.4, yellow to red).
- ○ **Use**: Suitable for titrations involving strong acids and strong bases.

3. **Indicators for Basic Range (pH > 7)**:

- ○ These indicators change color in basic conditions.
- ○ **Examples**: Phenolphthalein (pH 8.2 to 10.0, colorless to pink), Thymolphthalein (pH 9.3 to 10.5, colorless to blue).
- ○ **Use**: Suitable for titrations involving weak acids and strong bases.

Classification Based on Application in Titrations:

1. **Strong Acid vs. Strong Base**:

- The equivalence point is around pH 7, so indicators with a color change near this pH are suitable.
- **Examples**: Bromothymol Blue, Phenolphthalein.

2. **Strong Acid vs. Weak Base**:

- The equivalence point is below pH 7, so indicators that change color in the acidic range are used.
- **Examples**: Methyl Orange, Bromophenol Blue.

3. **Weak Acid vs. Strong Base**:

- The equivalence point is above pH 7, so indicators that change color in the basic range are appropriate.
- **Examples**: Phenolphthalein, Thymolphthalein.

4. **Weak Acid vs. Weak Base**:

- The equivalence point is difficult to determine accurately, so specific indicators for this titration type are not common.
- **Examples**: Mixed indicators or pH meters are often used.

Examples of Common Indicators:

1. **Phenolphthalein**:

- **pH Range**: 8.2 to 10.0
- **Color Change**: Colorless (HIn) to pink (In$^-$)
- **Use**: Suitable for titrations of strong bases against weak acids.

2. **Methyl Orange**:

- **pH Range**: 3.1 to 4.4
- **Color Change**: Red (HIn) to yellow (In-)
- **Use**: Suitable for titrations of strong acids against weak bases.

3. **Bromothymol Blue**:

- **pH Range**: 6.0 to 7.6
- **Color Change**: Yellow (HIn) to blue (In$^-$)
- **Use**: Suitable for titrations of strong acids against strong bases.

4. **Litmus**:

- **pH Range**: 4.5 to 8.3
- **Color Change**: Red in acidic conditions and blue in basic conditions.
- **Use**: General pH indicator for educational purposes.

5.2 Types of Acid-Base Titrations
5.2.1 Strong Acid-Strong Base Titrations

Introduction: Acid-base titrations are a fundamental analytical technique used to determine the concentration of an unknown acid or base by reacting it with a standard solution of a strong acid or base. Among the different types of acid-base titrations, strong acid-strong base titrations are the simplest and most straightforward. This type of titration involves a strong acid and a strong base, both of which completely dissociate in water, resulting in a clear and sharp endpoint.

Principle: In a strong acid-strong base titration, the strong acid and strong base react completely to form water and a salt. The equivalence point, where the moles of hydrogen ions (H$^+$) from the acid equal the moles of hydroxide ions (OH$^-$) from the base, occurs at pH 7.

Reaction Equation: The neutralization reaction between a strong acid and a strong base can be represented as follows:

HCl (aq)+NaOH (aq)$\rightarrow$NaCl (aq)+H2O (l)

Here, hydrochloric acid (HCl) reacts with sodium hydroxide (NaOH) to form sodium chloride (NaCl) and water (H2O).

Procedure:

1. **Preparation of the Solutions**:

- **Standard Solution (Titrant)**: Prepare a standard solution of a strong base, such as 0.1 M sodium hydroxide (NaOH).
- **Sample Solution (Analyte)**: Prepare the solution of the strong acid to be titrated, such as hydrochloric acid (HCl), of unknown concentration.

2. **Setting Up the Titration**:

   - **Burette**: Fill a burette with the standard NaOH solution. Record the initial volume.
   - **Erlenmeyer Flask**: Place a measured volume of the HCl solution in an Erlenmeyer flask. Add a few drops of a suitable indicator, such as phenolphthalein or bromothymol blue.

3. **Performing the Titration**:

   - Slowly add the NaOH solution from the burette to the HCl solution while continuously swirling the flask.
   - Observe the color change of the indicator. For phenolphthalein, the color changes from colorless to pink at the endpoint. For bromothymol blue, the color changes from yellow to blue.
   - As the endpoint approaches, add the NaOH solution dropwise to avoid overshooting the equivalence point.

4. **Determining the Endpoint**:

   - The endpoint is reached when the indicator changes color, indicating that the equivalence point has been achieved.
   - Record the final volume of NaOH in the burette.

5. **Calculations**:

   - Calculate the number of moles of NaOH added using the formula: Moles of NaOH=Molarity of NaOH×Volume of NaOH used (L)
   - Since the reaction ratio between HCl and NaOH is 1:1, the moles of HCl in the sample is equal to the moles of NaOH added.
   - Calculate the concentration of HCl using the formula: Concentration of HCl=Moles of HCl/Volume of HCl solution

Indicators Used:

- **Phenolphthalein**: Suitable for strong acid-strong base titrations due to its color change near pH 7 (colorless in acidic and neutral solutions, pink in basic solutions).

- **Bromothymol Blue**: Another suitable indicator, changing color from yellow in acidic solutions to blue in basic solutions.

5.2 Types of Acid-Base Titrations
5.2.2 Weak Acid-Strong Base Titrations

Introduction: Weak acid-strong base titrations involve the titration of a weak acid with a strong base. These titrations differ from strong acid-strong base titrations because the weak acid does not fully dissociate in water, which affects the shape of the titration curve and the pH at the equivalence point. Understanding these differences is crucial for selecting appropriate indicators and accurately determining the endpoint.

Principle: In a weak acid-strong base titration, the weak acid (HA) partially dissociates in water. When titrated with a strong base (such as NaOH), the strong base fully dissociates and neutralizes the weak acid, forming water and the conjugate base (A⁻) of the weak acid. The equivalence point occurs at a pH greater than 7 due to the formation of the conjugate base, which hydrolyzes to produce hydroxide ions (OH⁻).

Reaction Equation: The neutralization reaction between a weak acid and a strong base can be represented as follows:

$$HA\ (aq) + NaOH\ (aq) \rightarrow NaA\ (aq) + H_2O\ (l)$$

Here, acetic acid (HA) reacts with sodium hydroxide (NaOH) to form sodium acetate (NaA) and water (H_2O).

Procedure:

1. **Preparation of the Solutions**:

   - **Standard Solution (Titrant)**: Prepare a standard solution of a strong base, such as 0.1 M sodium hydroxide (NaOH).
   - **Sample Solution (Analyte)**: Prepare the solution of the weak acid to be titrated, such as acetic acid (CH_3COOH), of unknown concentration.

2. **Setting Up the Titration**:

   - **Burette**: Fill a burette with the standard NaOH solution. Record the initial volume.
   - **Erlenmeyer Flask**: Place a measured volume of the acetic acid solution in an Erlenmeyer flask. Add a few drops of a suitable

indicator, such as phenolphthalein or bromothymol blue.

3. **Performing the Titration**:

- Slowly add the NaOH solution from the burette to the acetic acid solution while continuously swirling the flask.
- Observe the color change of the indicator. For phenolphthalein, the color changes from colorless to pink at the endpoint. For bromothymol blue, the color changes from yellow to blue.
- As the endpoint approaches, add the NaOH solution dropwise to avoid overshooting the equivalence point.

4. **Determining the Endpoint**:

- The endpoint is reached when the indicator changes color, indicating that the equivalence point has been achieved.
- Record the final volume of NaOH in the burette.

5. **Calculations**:

- Calculate the number of moles of NaOH added using the formula: Moles of NaOH=Molarity of NaOH×Volume of NaOH used (L)
- Since the reaction ratio between HA and NaOH is 1:1, the moles of HA in the sample is equal to the moles of NaOH added.
- Calculate the concentration of HA using the formula: Concentration of HA=Moles of HAVolume of HA solution (L)

Indicators Used:

- **Phenolphthalein**: Suitable for weak acid-strong base titrations due to its color change in the basic pH range (colorless in acidic and neutral solutions, pink in basic solutions).
- **Bromothymol Blue**: Can also be used, changing color from yellow in acidic solutions to blue in basic solutions, but phenolphthalein is generally preferred for its clear color transition.

Titration Curve Characteristics:

- The pH increases gradually in the beginning as NaOH is added.
- Near the equivalence point, the pH rises sharply.
- The equivalence point is at a pH higher than 7 due to the basic nature of the conjugate base (acetate ion in this case).
- Beyond the equivalence point, the pH increases more slowly as excess NaOH is added.

5.2 Types of Acid-Base Titrations
5.2.3 Weak Base-Strong Acid Titrations

Introduction: Weak base-strong acid titrations involve the titration of a weak base with a strong acid. Unlike strong base-strong acid titrations, weak base-strong acid titrations are characterized by a more gradual pH change near the equivalence point, which occurs at a pH less than 7. This type of titration is important for accurately determining the concentration of weak bases.

Principle: In a weak base-strong acid titration, the weak base (B) partially dissociates in water. When titrated with a strong acid (such as HCl), the strong acid fully dissociates and neutralizes the weak base, forming water and the conjugate acid (BH^+). The equivalence point occurs at a pH less than 7 due to the formation of the conjugate acid, which can donate protons to water, increasing the concentration of hydrogen ions (H^+).

Reaction Equation: The neutralization reaction between a weak base and a strong acid can be represented as follows:

$$B\ (aq) + HCl\ (aq) \rightarrow BH^+(aq) + Cl^-(aq)$$

Here, ammonia (NH_3) reacts with hydrochloric acid (HCl) to form ammonium chloride (NH_4Cl).

Procedure:

1. **Preparation of the Solutions**:

   - **Standard Solution (Titrant)**: Prepare a standard solution of a strong acid, such as 0.1 M hydrochloric acid (HCl).
   - **Sample Solution (Analyte)**: Prepare the solution of the weak base to be titrated, such as ammonia (NH_3), of unknown concentration.

2. **Setting Up the Titration**:

- ○ **Burette**: Fill a burette with the standard HCl solution. Record the initial volume.
- ○ **Erlenmeyer Flask**: Place a measured volume of the ammonia solution in an Erlenmeyer flask. Add a few drops of a suitable indicator, such as methyl orange or bromophenol blue.

3. **Performing the Titration**:

- ○ Slowly add the HCl solution from the burette to the ammonia solution while continuously swirling the flask.
- ○ Observe the color change of the indicator. For methyl orange, the color changes from yellow to red at the endpoint. For bromophenol blue, the color changes from blue to yellow.
- ○ As the endpoint approaches, add the HCl solution dropwise to avoid overshooting the equivalence point.

4. **Determining the Endpoint**:

- ○ The endpoint is reached when the indicator changes color, indicating that the equivalence point has been achieved.
- ○ Record the final volume of HCl in the burette.

5. **Calculations**:

- ○ Calculate the number of moles of HCl added using the formula: Moles of HCl=Molarity of HCl×Volume of HCl used (L)
- ○ Since the reaction ratio between B and HCl is 1:1, the moles of B in the sample is equal to the moles of HCl added.
- ○ Calculate the concentration of B using the formula: Concentration of B=Moles of B / Volume of B solution (L)

Indicators Used:

- · **Methyl Orange**: Suitable for weak base-strong acid titrations due to its color change in the acidic pH range (yellow in basic and neutral solutions, red in acidic solutions).
- · **Bromophenol Blue**: Also suitable, changing color from blue in basic solutions to yellow in acidic solutions.

Titration Curve Characteristics:

- The pH decreases gradually in the beginning as HCl is added.
- Near the equivalence point, the pH drops sharply.
- The equivalence point is at a pH less than 7 due to the acidic nature of the conjugate acid (ammonium ion in this case).
- Beyond the equivalence point, the pH decreases more slowly as excess HCl is added.

5.2 Types of Acid-Base Titrations
5.2.4 Neutralization Curves

Introduction: Neutralization curves, also known as titration curves, graphically represent the change in pH of a solution as a titrant is added during a titration. These curves provide valuable insights into the behavior of acids and bases during titrations and help determine the equivalence point where neutralization occurs. The shape of the neutralization curve depends on the strength of the acid and base involved in the titration.

Principle: The neutralization curve plots pH on the y-axis against the volume of titrant added on the x-axis. The equivalence point is where the number of moles of acid equals the number of moles of base, resulting in a neutral solution for strong acid-strong base titrations or a slightly acidic or basic solution for weak acid-strong base or weak base-strong acid titrations.

Types of Neutralization Curves:

1. **Strong Acid-Strong Base Titration**:

   - **Example**: Hydrochloric acid (HCl) titrated with sodium hydroxide (NaOH).
   - **Curve Characteristics**:

     - Starts at a low pH (strong acid).
     - pH rises gradually as NaOH is added.
     - Sharp, almost vertical increase in pH at the equivalence point (around pH 7).
     - pH levels off at a high pH after the equivalence point.

   - **Equivalence Point**: pH 7.

2. **Weak Acid-Strong Base Titration**:

   - **Example**: Acetic acid (CH_3COOH) titrated with sodium hydroxide (NaOH).
   - **Curve Characteristics**:

     - Starts at a higher pH compared to a strong acid (weak acid).
     - pH rises gradually, with a buffer region where the pH changes slowly.
     - Sharp increase in pH near the equivalence point (above pH 7).
     - pH levels off at a high pH after the equivalence point.

   - **Equivalence Point**: pH > 7.

3. **Weak Base-Strong Acid Titration**:

   - **Example**: Ammonia (NH_3) titrated with hydrochloric acid (HCl).
   - **Curve Characteristics**:

     - Starts at a higher pH (weak base).
     - pH decreases gradually as HCl is added, with a buffer region where the pH changes slowly.
     - Sharp decrease in pH near the equivalence point (below pH 7).
     - pH levels off at a low pH after the equivalence point.

   - **Equivalence Point**: pH < 7.

4. **Weak Acid-Weak Base Titration**:

   - **Example**: Acetic acid (CH_3COOH) titrated with ammonia (NH_3).
   - **Curve Characteristics**:

     - Starts at a moderate pH (weak acid).
     - pH changes gradually throughout the titration.
     - No sharp change in pH at the equivalence point.
     - Equivalence point can be difficult to identify.

- **Equivalence Point**: pH depends on the relative strengths of the weak acid and weak base.

Detailed Example of a Strong Acid-Strong Base Titration:

1. **Initial Setup**:

   - **Titrant**: 0.1 M NaOH.
   - **Analyte**: 25.0 mL of 0.1 M HCl.

2. **Titration Process**:

   - As NaOH is added to the HCl solution, the pH is measured at regular intervals.

3. **Plotting the Curve**:

   - **Initial pH**: Before any NaOH is added, the pH of 0.1 M HCl is approximately 1.
   - **Adding NaOH**: The pH gradually increases as NaOH neutralizes the HCl.
   - **Near Equivalence Point**: Around 25.0 mL of NaOH, the pH rises sharply.
   - **At Equivalence Point**: pH is approximately 7.
   - **Beyond Equivalence Point**: Adding more NaOH increases the pH rapidly, leveling off at a high pH.

Indicators and Their Use:

- **Strong Acid-Strong Base**: Phenolphthalein or bromothymol blue, with a sharp color change at pH 7.
- **Weak Acid-Strong Base**: Phenolphthalein, with a color change in the basic range.
- **Weak Base-Strong Acid**: Methyl orange or bromophenol blue, with a color change in the acidic range.
- **Weak Acid-Weak Base**: No sharp endpoint; use a pH meter or a mixed indicator.

Here are the simple plots for the neutralization curves:

1. **Strong Acid-Strong Base Titration (HCl and NaOH):**

   - The pH starts at 1 (strong acid) and rises sharply near the equivalence point (around 25 mL of NaOH added), reaching a pH of 7. After the equivalence point, the pH levels off at around 13.

2. **Weak Acid-Strong Base Titration (Acetic Acid and NaOH):**

   - The pH starts at 3 (weak acid) and rises gradually with a buffer region where the pH changes slowly. Near the equivalence point (around 25 mL of NaOH added), the pH rises sharply, reaching a value above 7. After the equivalence point, the pH levels off at around 13.

3. **Weak Base-Strong Acid Titration (Ammonia and HCl):**

   - The pH starts at 11 (weak base) and decreases gradually with a buffer region where the pH changes slowly. Near the equivalence point (around 25 mL of HCl added), the pH drops sharply, reaching a value below 7. After the equivalence point, the pH levels off at around 1.

These curves illustrate the characteristic pH changes during different types of acid-base titrations, helping to identify the equivalence points and select appropriate indicators for accurate titration results.

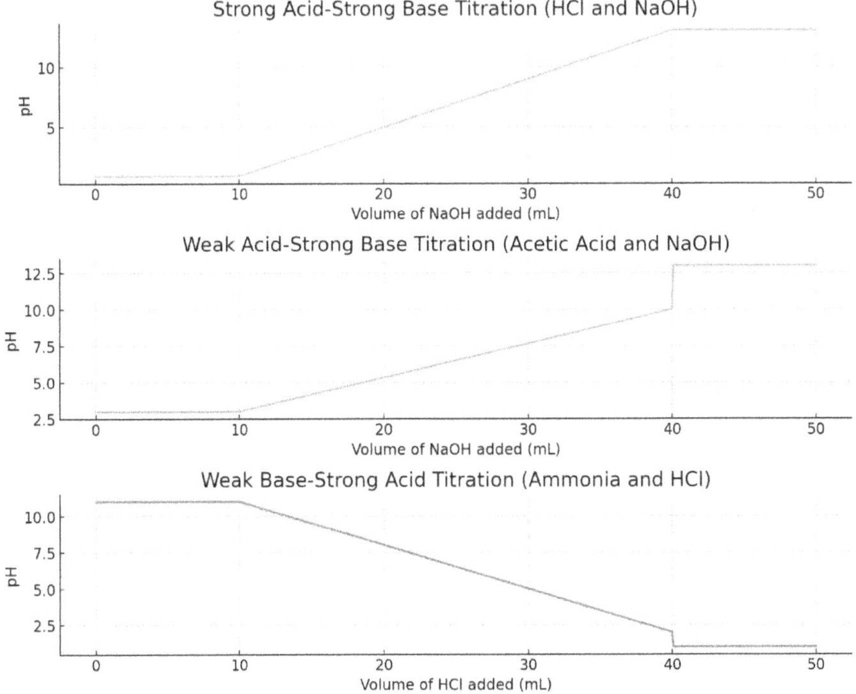

Neutralization curves

5.3 Non-Aqueous Titrations

5.3.1 Solvents Used in Non-Aqueous Titrations

Introduction: Non-aqueous titrations are performed in solvents other than water. These titrations are used when the analyte or titrant is not soluble or stable in water, or when water interferes with the reaction. The choice of solvent is critical as it can influence the titration's course, the solubility of the analyte and titrant, and the accuracy of the endpoint detection.

Solvents Used in Non-Aqueous Titrations:

1. **Protic Solvents:**

   ○ **Definition**: Protic solvents are those that have a hydrogen atom attached to an electronegative atom (such as oxygen or nitrogen) and can donate protons (H^+).

- ○ **Examples**: Methanol, ethanol, acetic acid, formic acid.
- ○ **Characteristics**:

  - Capable of forming hydrogen bonds.
  - Can act as acids or bases.
  - Useful in titrations where the analyte is more soluble in an acidic or basic medium.

- ○ **Applications**: Often used in titrations of weak bases or in acidimetry where a strong acidic environment is needed.

2. **Aprotic Solvents**:

- ○ **Definition**: Aprotic solvents do not have hydrogen atoms that can form hydrogen bonds. They cannot donate protons.
- ○ **Examples**: Dimethyl sulfoxide (DMSO), acetonitrile, acetone, dimethylformamide (DMF), tetrahydrofuran (THF).
- ○ **Characteristics**:

  - Do not participate in hydrogen bonding.
  - Generally have high dielectric constants, making them good solvents for ionic species.
  - Inert to many chemical reactions.

- ○ **Applications**: Suitable for titrations involving strong acids or bases, and for substances that require a non-reactive medium.

3. **Mixed Solvents**:

- ○ **Definition**: Mixed solvents are combinations of two or more solvents, tailored to achieve the desired solubility and reactivity properties.
- ○ **Examples**: Mixtures of methanol and chloroform, acetonitrile and methanol.
- ○ **Characteristics**:

  - Can be customized to balance solubility, dielectric constant, and reactivity.

- Useful for titrations where a single solvent does not provide optimal conditions.

- **Applications**: Employed in complex titrations where a balance of solvent properties is required for accurate results.

Specific Solvents and Their Applications:

1. **Methanol (CH$_3$OH)**:

   - **Characteristics**: Protic solvent, polar, miscible with water.
   - **Applications**: Used in the titration of weak bases and in Karl Fischer titration for water determination.
   - **Advantages**: Good solvent for a wide range of substances, enhances the solubility of many organic compounds.

2. **Dimethyl Sulfoxide (DMSO, (CH$_3$)$_2$SO)**:

   - **Characteristics**: Aprotic solvent, highly polar, high boiling point.
   - **Applications**: Used in the titration of weak acids and bases, especially in organometallic chemistry.
   - **Advantages**: Excellent solvent for polar compounds, stable under a wide range of conditions.

3. **Acetonitrile (CH$_3$CN)**:

   - **Characteristics**: Aprotic solvent, polar, low viscosity.
   - **Applications**: Commonly used in titrations involving perchloric acid, especially in pharmaceutical analysis.
   - **Advantages**: Good solvent for ionic and polar compounds, high dielectric constant enhances solubility of salts.

4. **Dimethylformamide (DMF, HCON(CH$_3$)$_2$)**:

   - **Characteristics**: Aprotic solvent, polar, high boiling point.
   - **Applications**: Suitable for titrations of weak acids and bases, and in the determination of acidic and basic pharmaceuticals.

- ○ **Advantages**: Solvent for a wide range of organic and inorganic compounds, stable under acidic and basic conditions.

5. **Glacial Acetic Acid (CH$_3$COOH):**

- ○ **Characteristics**: Protic solvent, polar, strong acid.
- ○ **Applications**: Used in the titration of amines and other weak bases.
- ○ **Advantages**: Enhances the solubility of basic compounds, provides a strong acidic environment.

Example of a Non-Aqueous Titration:
Titration of a Weak Base (Pyridine) with Perchloric Acid in Glacial Acetic Acid:

1. **Preparation:**

- ○ **Titrant**: 0.1 M perchloric acid in glacial acetic acid.
- ○ **Analyte**: Pyridine solution in glacial acetic acid.

2. **Procedure:**

- ○ Add a few drops of crystal violet as an indicator to the pyridine solution.
- ○ Titrate with the perchloric acid solution.
- ○ The endpoint is indicated by a color change from violet to green.

Type of Titration	Description	pH at Equivalence Point
Strong Acid-Strong Base	Sharp change in pH at equivalence point.	pH = 7
Weak Acid-Strong Base	Gradual change in pH, equivalence point above 7.	pH > 7
Strong Acid-Weak Base	Gradual change in pH, equivalence point below 7.	pH < 7
Weak Acid-Weak Base	Very gradual change in pH, difficult to pinpoint.	Varies depending on relative strengths.

Neutralization Curves

5.3 Non-Aqueous Titrations
5.3.2 Acidimetry in Non-Aqueous Media

Introduction: Acidimetry in non-aqueous media involves the titration of weak acids with strong bases in solvents other than water. This method is particularly useful for acids that are insoluble or unstable in aqueous solutions, or when water interferes with the titration process. Non-aqueous acidimetry provides a broader range of analytical possibilities, especially for organic acids and pharmaceuticals.

Principle: In non-aqueous acidimetry, a weak acid (analyte) is titrated with a strong base (titrant) in a non-aqueous solvent. The solvent plays a crucial role in determining the ionization and reactivity of the acid and base. The endpoint of the titration is usually detected using a suitable indicator that changes color at the equivalence point.

Solvents Used in Non-Aqueous Acidimetry:

1. **Glacial Acetic Acid (CH_3COOH)**:

   - **Characteristics**: Protic solvent, polar, strong acid.
   - **Application**: Suitable for titrations of weak organic bases.
   - **Advantage**: Enhances the solubility of basic compounds and provides a strong acidic environment.

2. **Acetonitrile (CH_3CN)**:

   - **Characteristics**: Aprotic solvent, polar, low viscosity.
   - **Application**: Commonly used for titrations involving perchloric acid.
   - **Advantage**: Good solvent for ionic and polar compounds, high dielectric constant enhances solubility of salts.

3. **Dimethylformamide (DMF, $HCON(CH_3)_2$)**:

   - **Characteristics**: Aprotic solvent, polar, high boiling point.
   - **Application**: Suitable for titrations of weak acids and bases.
   - **Advantage**: Solvent for a wide range of organic and inorganic compounds, stable under acidic and basic conditions.

Procedure for Non-Aqueous Acidimetry:

1. **Preparation of Solutions**:

   - **Titrant**: Prepare a standard solution of a strong base, such as 0.1 M sodium methoxide ($NaOCH_3$) or potassium hydroxide (KOH) in methanol.
   - **Analyte**: Dissolve the weak acid to be titrated in the chosen non-aqueous solvent.

2. **Indicator Selection**:

   - Choose an appropriate indicator that changes color at the equivalence point in the non-aqueous medium.
   - Common indicators: Crystal violet (color change: violet to green), thymol blue (color change: yellow to blue).

3. **Titration Setup**:

   - Fill a burette with the standard base solution.
   - Place the weak acid solution in an Erlenmeyer flask or titration vessel.
   - Add a few drops of the selected indicator to the analyte solution.

4. **Performing the Titration**:

   - Slowly add the base solution from the burette to the acid solution while continuously swirling the flask.
   - Observe the color change of the indicator as the titrant is added.
   - As the endpoint approaches, add the base solution dropwise to avoid overshooting the equivalence point.

5. **Determining the Endpoint**:

   - The endpoint is reached when the indicator changes color, signaling that the equivalence point has been achieved.
   - Record the final volume of the base solution in the burette.

Example of Non-Aqueous Acidimetry:
Titration of Benzoic Acid with Sodium Methoxide in Methanol:

1. **Preparation**:

   - **Titrant**: 0.1 M sodium methoxide ($NaOCH_3$) in methanol.
   - **Analyte**: Benzoic acid solution in methanol.

2. **Procedure**:

   - Add a few drops of crystal violet as an indicator to the benzoic acid solution.
   - Titrate with the sodium methoxide solution.
   - The endpoint is indicated by a color change from violet to green.

5.3 Non-Aqueous Titrations
5.3.3 Alkalimetry in Non-Aqueous Media

Introduction: Alkalimetry in non-aqueous media involves the titration of weak bases with strong acids in solvents other than water. This technique is particularly useful for bases that are insoluble or unstable in aqueous solutions, or when water interferes with the titration process. Non-aqueous alkalimetry expands the analytical capabilities for various organic and pharmaceutical compounds.

Principle: In non-aqueous alkalimetry, a weak base (analyte) is titrated with a strong acid (titrant) in a non-aqueous solvent. The solvent plays a crucial role in determining the ionization and reactivity of the base and acid. The endpoint of the titration is usually detected using a suitable indicator that changes color at the equivalence point.

Solvents Used in Non-Aqueous Alkalimetry:

1. **Glacial Acetic Acid (CH_3COOH)**:

   - **Characteristics**: Protic solvent, polar, strong acid.
   - **Application**: Suitable for titrations of weak organic bases.
   - **Advantage**: Enhances the solubility of basic compounds and provides a strong acidic environment.

2. **Acetonitrile (CH_3CN)**:

   - **Characteristics**: Aprotic solvent, polar, low viscosity.
   - **Application**: Commonly used for titrations involving perchloric acid.

- **Advantage**: Good solvent for ionic and polar compounds, high dielectric constant enhances solubility of salts.

3. **Dimethylformamide (DMF, HCON(CH$_3$)$_2$):**

   - **Characteristics**: Aprotic solvent, polar, high boiling point.
   - **Application**: Suitable for titrations of weak acids and bases.
   - **Advantage**: Solvent for a wide range of organic and inorganic compounds, stable under acidic and basic conditions.

Procedure for Non-Aqueous Alkalimetry:

1. **Preparation of Solutions:**

   - **Titrant**: Prepare a standard solution of a strong acid, such as 0.1 M perchloric acid (HClO$_4$) in acetic acid or acetonitrile.
   - **Analyte**: Dissolve the weak base to be titrated in the chosen non-aqueous solvent.

2. **Indicator Selection:**

   - Choose an appropriate indicator that changes color at the equivalence point in the non-aqueous medium.
   - Common indicators: Crystal violet (color change: violet to green), thymol blue (color change: yellow to blue).

3. **Titration Setup:**

   - Fill a burette with the standard acid solution.
   - Place the weak base solution in an Erlenmeyer flask or titration vessel.
   - Add a few drops of the selected indicator to the analyte solution.

4. **Performing the Titration:**

   - Slowly add the acid solution from the burette to the base solution while continuously swirling the flask.
   - Observe the color change of the indicator as the titrant is added.

- ○ As the endpoint approaches, add the acid solution dropwise to avoid overshooting the equivalence point.

5. **Determining the Endpoint**:

- ○ The endpoint is reached when the indicator changes color, signaling that the equivalence point has been achieved.
- ○ Record the final volume of the acid solution in the burette.

Calculations:

- Calculate the number of moles of the acid added using the formula: Moles of acid=Molarity of acid×Volume of acid used (L)
- Since the reaction ratio between the base and acid is 1:1, the moles of base in the sample are equal to the moles of the acid added.
- Calculate the concentration of the base using the formula: Concentration of base=Moles of base / Volume of base solution (L)

Example of Non-Aqueous Alkalimetry:
Titration of Pyridine with Perchloric Acid in Acetic Acid:

1. **Preparation**:

- ○ **Titrant**: 0.1 M perchloric acid ($HClO_4$) in acetic acid.
- ○ **Analyte**: Pyridine solution in acetic acid.

2. **Procedure**:

- ○ Add a few drops of crystal violet as an indicator to the pyridine solution.
- ○ Titrate with the perchloric acid solution.
- ○ The endpoint is indicated by a color change from violet to green.

3. **Calculation**:

- ○ Determine the volume of perchloric acid used to reach the endpoint.
- ○ Calculate the concentration of pyridine using the titration formula: Moles of pyridine=Moles of perchloric acid=Molarity of

$HClO_4 \times$ Volume of

5.3 Non-Aqueous Titrations
5.3.4 Estimation of Sodium Benzoate

Introduction: Sodium benzoate is a commonly used preservative in the pharmaceutical and food industries. Its estimation is crucial for quality control and regulatory compliance. Non-aqueous titration provides an effective method for the precise estimation of sodium benzoate, especially when the compound's solubility or stability in water is limited.

Principle: The estimation of sodium benzoate can be carried out using non-aqueous titration with perchloric acid as the titrant in an acetic acid medium. The endpoint of the titration is determined using an appropriate indicator that changes color at the equivalence point.

Reaction Equation: The reaction between sodium benzoate ($NaC_7H_5O_2$) and perchloric acid (HClO4) in acetic acid medium can be represented as follows:

$$NaC_7H_5O_2 + HClO_4 \rightarrow C_7H_6O_2 + NaClO_4$$

Procedure for Estimation of Sodium Benzoate:

1. **Preparation of Solutions**:

   - **Titrant**: Prepare a standard solution of 0.1 M perchloric acid ($HClO_4$) in glacial acetic acid.
   - **Sample Solution**: Accurately weigh the sodium benzoate sample and dissolve it in glacial acetic acid.

2. **Indicator Selection**:

   - Choose an appropriate indicator that changes color at the equivalence point in the non-aqueous medium. Crystal violet is commonly used as an indicator for this titration.
   - **Indicator**: Crystal violet (color change: violet to green).

3. **Titration Setup**:

   - Fill a burette with the standard perchloric acid solution.
   - Place the sodium benzoate solution in an Erlenmeyer flask or titration vessel.

- Add a few drops of crystal violet indicator to the analyte solution.

4. Performing the Titration:

- Slowly add the perchloric acid solution from the burette to the sodium benzoate solution while continuously swirling the flask.
- Observe the color change of the indicator as the titrant is added.
- As the endpoint approaches, add the perchloric acid solution dropwise to avoid overshooting the equivalence point.

5. Determining the Endpoint:

- The endpoint is reached when the indicator changes color from violet to green, indicating that the equivalence point has been achieved.
- Record the final volume of the perchloric acid solution in the burette.

Precautions:

- Ensure all glassware and reagents are clean and free from contaminants.
- Handle perchloric acid with care, as it is a strong acid and can be hazardous.
- Perform the titration under consistent lighting conditions to ensure accurate visual comparison.
- Properly dispose of waste according to safety regulations due to the use of hazardous chemicals.

5.3 Non-Aqueous Titrations
5.3.5 Estimation of Ephedrine HCl

Introduction: Ephedrine HCl is a commonly used medication in treating asthma, nasal congestion, and other respiratory conditions. Accurate estimation of ephedrine HCl is crucial for quality control in pharmaceutical formulations. Non-aqueous titration provides an effective method for its precise estimation, especially when the compound's solubility or stability in water is limited.

Principle: The estimation of ephedrine HCl can be carried out using non-aqueous titration with perchloric acid as the titrant in an anhydrous acetic acid medium. The endpoint of the titration is determined using an appropriate indicator that changes color at the equivalence point.

Reaction Equation: The reaction between ephedrine HCl ($C_{10}H_{15}NO \cdot HCl$) and perchloric acid ($HClO_4$) in an acetic acid medium can be represented as follows:

$$C_{10}H_{15}NO \cdot HCl + HClO_4 \rightarrow C_{10}H_{15}NO \cdot HClO_4 + HCl$$

Procedure for Estimation of Ephedrine HCl:

1. **Preparation of Solutions**:

   - **Titrant**: Prepare a standard solution of 0.1 M perchloric acid ($HClO_4$) in glacial acetic acid.
   - **Sample Solution**: Accurately weigh the ephedrine HCl sample and dissolve it in glacial acetic acid.

2. **Indicator Selection**:

   - Choose an appropriate indicator that changes color at the equivalence point in the non-aqueous medium. Crystal violet is commonly used as an indicator for this titration.
   - **Indicator**: Crystal violet (color change: violet to green).

3. **Titration Setup**:

   - Fill a burette with the standard perchloric acid solution.
   - Place the ephedrine HCl solution in an Erlenmeyer flask or titration vessel.
   - Add a few drops of crystal violet indicator to the analyte solution.

4. **Performing the Titration**:

   - Slowly add the perchloric acid solution from the burette to the ephedrine HCl solution while continuously swirling the flask.
   - Observe the color change of the indicator as the titrant is added.
   - As the endpoint approaches, add the perchloric acid solution dropwise to avoid overshooting the equivalence point.

5. **Determining the Endpoint**:

- ○ The endpoint is reached when the indicator changes color from violet to green, indicating that the equivalence point has been achieved.
- ○ Record the final volume of the perchloric acid solution in the burette.

Precautions:

- Ensure all glassware and reagents are clean and free from contaminants.
- Handle perchloric acid with care, as it is a strong acid and can be hazardous.
- Perform the titration under consistent lighting conditions to ensure accurate visual comparison.
- Properly dispose of waste according to safety regulations due to the use of hazardous chemicals.

Type	Description	Example Reaction
Acidimetry in Non-Aqueous Media	Titration of acids using non-aqueous solvents.	$RCOOH + EtOH \rightarrow RCOOEt + H_2O$
Alkalimetry in Non-Aqueous Media	Titration of bases using non-aqueous solvents.	$RNH_2 + EtOH \rightarrow RNH_3OEt$
Estimation of Sodium Benzoate	Sodium benzoate titrated in non-aqueous medium.	$C_6H_5COONa + H_2SO_4 \rightarrow C_6H_5COOH + NaHSO_4$
Estimation of Ephedrine HCl	Ephedrine HCl titrated in non-aqueous medium.	$C_10H_15ONH_3Cl + EtOH \rightarrow C_10H_15OEt + NH_4Cl$

Non-Aqueous Titrations

SIX
PRECIPITATION TITRATIONS

Introduction to Precipitation Titrations

Precipitation titrations are a type of volumetric analysis in which the analyte reacts with a titrant to form an insoluble precipitate. This technique is widely used in quantitative chemical analysis to determine the concentration of a particular ion in a solution. The endpoint of the titration is typically indicated by the formation of a precipitate or a color change due to the presence of an indicator.

Principle of Precipitation Titrations

The principle of precipitation titrations is based on the formation of an insoluble compound when the titrant is added to the analyte solution. The reaction between the analyte and the titrant proceeds until one of the reactants is completely consumed, resulting in the formation of a precipitate. The amount of titrant required to reach the endpoint is used to calculate the concentration of the analyte in the solution.

Common Types of Precipitation Titrations

1. **Mohr's Method**: This method involves the titration of chloride ions with a silver nitrate solution. The endpoint is indicated by the formation of a red-brown precipitate of silver chromate when all the chloride ions have reacted.

2. **Volhard's Method**: This method is used to determine halide ions (e.g., Cl^-, Br^-, I^-) by back-titration with thiocyanate after adding an excess of silver nitrate. The excess silver ions are titrated with ammonium thiocyanate, and the endpoint is indicated by the formation of a red-colored complex

with iron(III) ions.

3. **Fajans Method**: This method uses an adsorption indicator that changes color at the endpoint. The titrant is added until the precipitate adsorbs the indicator, resulting in a color change.

Applications of Precipitation Titrations

Precipitation titrations are commonly used in various fields such as environmental analysis, pharmaceuticals, food industry, and water treatment. They are particularly useful for:

- Determining the concentration of halide ions (chloride, bromide, iodide) in water samples.
- Analyzing the purity of pharmaceutical compounds.
- Measuring the hardness of water by determining the concentration of calcium and magnesium ions.

Advantages of Precipitation Titrations

- **High Precision**: These titrations can provide highly precise and accurate results when properly executed.
- **Simple Equipment**: The method requires relatively simple laboratory equipment, making it accessible for many laboratories.
- **Versatility**: Precipitation titrations can be adapted for a wide range of analytes by selecting appropriate titrants and indicators.

Limitations of Precipitation Titrations

- **Endpoint Detection**: Accurate detection of the endpoint can sometimes be challenging, especially if the precipitate forms slowly or is colloidal.
- **Interference**: The presence of other ions in the solution can interfere with the formation of the precipitate, affecting the accuracy of the titration.
- **Solubility Issues**: The solubility of the precipitate can affect the titration's accuracy, as highly soluble precipitates may not fully precipitate out of the solution.

6.1 Principles of Precipitation Titrations
6.1.1 Solubility Product

Introduction: The solubility product (Ksp) is an equilibrium constant that applies to the solubility of sparingly soluble salts. It is a critical concept in precipitation titrations, which are used to determine the concentration of ions in a solution by forming an insoluble precipitate.

Principle: The solubility product constant (Ksp) is defined for a sparingly soluble salt that dissociates in water into its constituent ions. For a general salt ABABAB that dissociates as:

$AB(s) \rightleftharpoons A^+(aq) + B^-(aq)$ The solubility product expression is:

$Ksp = [A^+][B^-]$

Where:

- $[A^+]$ is the molar concentration of the cation.
- $[B^-]$ the molar concentration of the anion.

The value of Ksp is constant for a given salt at a particular temperature.

Application: In precipitation titrations, the endpoint is reached when the ion product of the reacting ions equals the Ksp causing the formation of a precipitate. The titration can be monitored by using indicators that signal the formation of a precipitate or by observing the solution's turbidity.

Example: Consider the titration of silver nitrate ($AgNO_3$) with sodium chloride (NaCl). The reaction is:

$AgNO_3 + NaCl \rightarrow AgCl\downarrow + NaNO_3$

The solubility product of silver chloride (AgCl) is:

$Ksp = [Ag^+][Cl^-] = 1.8 \times 10{-}10$

At the endpoint, the concentrations of Ag^+ and Cl^- in the solution will be such that their product equals Ksp.

6.1.2 Common Ion Effect

Introduction: The common ion effect is observed when a salt containing an ion that is already present in the solution is added, shifting the equilibrium and affecting the solubility of the original salt. This effect is vital in precipitation titrations as it influences the point at which precipitation begins.

Principle: When a common ion is added to a solution, the solubility of the salt containing that ion is decreased. This is explained by Le Chatelier's principle, which states that the addition of a common ion shifts the equilibrium position to reduce the ionization of the weak electrolyte.

Mechanism:

1. **Ionization of Weak Electrolyte**: Consider a weak electrolyte HA ionizing in water:

$$HA \rightleftharpoons H^+ + A^-$$

1. **Addition of Common Ion**: Adding a salt like NaA increases the concentration of A–ions in the solution.
2. **Shift in Equilibrium**: The increased concentration of A– shifts the equilibrium to the left, reducing the ionization of HA:

$$HA \rightleftharpoons H^+ + A^-$$

Effect on Solubility: This principle can be applied to the solubility of salts. For instance, adding NaCl to a solution of AgCl will increase the concentration of Cl–ions, decreasing the solubility of AgCl.

Applications in Analytical Chemistry:

1. **Buffer Solutions**: Buffers rely on the common ion effect to maintain pH stability. A buffer solution of acetic acid and sodium acetate uses the common ion effect to suppress the ionization of acetic acid.
2. **pH Control**: The common ion effect helps in controlling the pH during titrations and other analytical processes by reducing the ionization of weak acids or bases.
3. **Precipitation Reactions**: In qualitative and quantitative analysis, the common ion effect is used to selectively precipitate ions from a solution. For instance, in gravimetric analysis, adding a common ion can facilitate the precipitation of a specific salt.

6.2 Methods of Precipitation Titrations
6.2.1 Mohr's Method

Introduction: Mohr's method is a classic precipitation titration technique used to determine the concentration of chloride ions in a solution. This method involves the titration of chloride ions with a standard solution of silver nitrate ($AgNO_3$), using potassium chromate (K_2CrO_4) as an indicator. The endpoint is indicated by the formation of a red-brown precipitate of silver chromate (Ag_2CrO_4).

Principle: The principle of Mohr's method is based on the precipitation of silver chloride (AgCl) when silver nitrate is added to a solution containing chloride ions. The titration proceeds until all chloride ions are precipitated as silver chloride. At the endpoint, any additional silver nitrate reacts with the potassium chromate indicator to form a red-brown precipitate of silver chromate.

Reaction Equations:

1. Precipitation of silver chloride: $Cl^-(aq)+Ag^+(aq)\rightarrow AgCl(s)\backslash$
2. Formation of silver chromate at the endpoint: $2Ag^+(aq)+CrO_4^{2-}(aq)\rightarrow Ag_2CrO_4(s)$ **Procedure for Mohr's Method**:

1. **Preparation of Solutions**:

    - **Titrant**: Prepare a standard solution of silver nitrate ($AgNO_3$).
    - **Sample Solution**: Prepare the chloride ion solution to be analyzed.
    - **Indicator**: Prepare a 5% potassium chromate (K_2CrO_4) solution.

2. **Indicator Addition**:

    - Add a few drops of the potassium chromate indicator to the sample solution. The solution will turn yellow due to the chromate ions.

3. **Titration Setup**:

    - Fill a burette with the standard silver nitrate solution.
    - Place the chloride ion solution in an Erlenmeyer flask or titration vessel.
    - Add the potassium chromate indicator to the chloride ion solution.

4. **Performing the Titration**:

    - Slowly add the silver nitrate solution from the burette to the chloride ion solution while continuously swirling the flask.
    - Observe the color change of the solution. Initially, a white precipitate of silver chloride will form.
    - As the endpoint approaches, add the silver nitrate solution dropwise to avoid overshooting the equivalence point.

5. **Determining the Endpoint**:

- The endpoint is reached when a permanent red-brown color appears, indicating the formation of silver chromate (Ag_2CrO_4).
- Record the final volume of the silver nitrate solution in the burette.

6. **Calculations**:

  - Calculate the concentration of chloride ions using the formula: Concentration of Cl^-=Moles of Cl^-/Volume of Cl^- solution (L)
  - **Precautions**:

- Ensure all glassware and reagents are clean and free from contaminants.
- Handle silver nitrate with care, as it can stain skin and clothing.
- Perform the titration under consistent lighting conditions to ensure accurate visual comparison.
- Properly dispose of waste according to safety regulations due to the use of hazardous chemicals.

Applications of Mohr's Method:

- Determination of chloride ion concentration in water samples.
- Analysis of chloride content in pharmaceutical preparations.
- Quality control in the food and beverage industry.

6.2 Methods of Precipitation Titrations

6.2.2 Volhard's Method

Introduction: Volhard's method is a classical titration technique used for the determination of halide ions (such as chloride, bromide, and iodide) and other anions (such as thiocyanate) in a solution. This method involves the formation of a precipitate using a standard silver nitrate solution, followed by the back-titration of the excess silver ions with a thiocyanate solution using iron(III) ammonium sulfate as an indicator.

Principle: Volhard's method is based on the precipitation of halide ions with silver nitrate to form insoluble silver halides. The excess silver nitrate is then titrated with a standard thiocyanate solution. The endpoint is indicated by the formation of a red complex between iron(III) ions and thiocyanate ions.

Reaction Equations:

1. Precipitation of halide ions with silver nitrate: $AgNO_3 + X^- \rightarrow AgX\downarrow + NO_3^{3-}$
2. Back-titration of excess silver ions with thiocyanate: $Ag^+ + SCN^- \rightarrow AgSCN\downarrow$
3. Formation of the red complex at the endpoint: $Fe^{3+} + 3SCN^- \rightarrow Fe(SCN)_3$

Procedure for Volhard's Method:

1. **Preparation of Solutions:**

   - **Titrant 1**: Prepare a standard solution of silver nitrate ($AgNO_3$).
   - **Titrant 2**: Prepare a standard solution of ammonium thiocyanate (NH_4SCN).
   - **Sample Solution**: Prepare the halide ion solution to be analyzed.
   - **Indicator**: Prepare a solution of iron(III) ammonium sulfate (ferric ammonium sulfate).

2. **Precipitation of Halide Ions:**

   - Add an excess amount of standard silver nitrate solution to the halide ion solution. The halide ions will precipitate as silver halides: $X^- + AgNO_3 \rightarrow AgX\downarrow + NO_3^{3-}$

3. **Removal of Precipitate:**

   - Filter the solution to remove the precipitated silver halides (AgX). The filtrate contains excess unreacted silver ions (Ag^+).

4. **Back-Titration with Thiocyanate:**

   - Add a few drops of the iron(III) ammonium sulfate indicator to the filtrate. The solution will turn yellow due to the presence of Fe^{3+} ions.
   - Titrate the excess silver ions in the filtrate with the standard ammonium thiocyanate solution. The thiocyanate ions will react with the silver ions to form a white precipitate of silver thiocyanate ($AgSCN$): $Ag^+ + SCN^- \rightarrow AgSCN\downarrow$ As the endpoint is approached, add the thiocyanate solution dropwise to avoid overshooting the equivalence point.

5. **Determining the Endpoint:**

- The endpoint is reached when a permanent red color appears, indicating the formation of the red complex between iron(III) ions and excess thiocyanate ions: $Fe^{3+}+3SCN- \rightarrow Fe(SCN)_3$
- Record the final volume of the ammonium thiocyanate solution in the burette.

Precautions:

- Ensure all glassware and reagents are clean and free from contaminants.
- Handle silver nitrate with care, as it can stain skin and clothing.
- Perform the titration under consistent lighting conditions to ensure accurate visual comparison.
- Properly dispose of waste according to safety regulations due to the use of hazardous chemicals.

Applications of Volhard's Method:

- Determination of chloride, bromide, and iodide ion concentrations in water samples.
- Analysis of thiocyanate in biological fluids and industrial samples.
- Quality control in the pharmaceutical industry for halide content.

6.2 Methods of Precipitation Titrations
6.2.3 Modified Volhard's Method

Introduction: The modified Volhard's method is a variation of the classical Volhard's method used to determine the concentration of halide ions in a solution. This modification involves conducting the titration in an acidic medium to prevent the precipitation of silver salts other than the target silver halide. This method provides greater accuracy in the presence of interfering ions.

Principle: The modified Volhard's method involves the addition of an excess amount of silver nitrate to the halide solution, followed by the addition of an acid (usually nitric acid) to prevent the precipitation of any interfering silver salts. The excess silver nitrate is then back-titrated with a standard thiocyanate solution using iron(III) ammonium sulfate as an indicator.

Reaction Equations:

1. Precipitation of halide ions with silver nitrate: $X^-(aq)+Ag^+(aq)\rightarrow AgX(s)$ (where $X^- = Cl^-, Br^-, I^-$)
2. Back-titration of excess silver ions with thiocyanate: $Ag^+(aq)+SCN^-(aq)\rightarrow AgSCN(s)$
3. Formation of the red complex at the endpoint: $Fe^{3+}(aq)+3SCN^-(aq)\rightarrow Fe(SCN)_3(aq)$ **Procedure for Modified Volhard's Method:**

1. **Preparation of Solutions:**

   - **Titrant 1:** Prepare a standard solution of silver nitrate ($AgNO_3$), typically 0.1 M.
   - **Titrant 2:** Prepare a standard solution of ammonium thiocyanate (NH_4SCN), typically 0.1 M.
   - **Sample Solution:** Prepare the halide ion solution to be analyzed.
   - **Indicator:** Prepare a solution of iron(III) ammonium sulfate (ferric ammonium sulfate).
   - **Acid:** Nitric acid (HNO_3) to create an acidic medium.

2. **Precipitation of Halide Ions:**

   - Add a known excess amount of standard silver nitrate solution to the halide ion solution. The halide ions will precipitate as silver halides: $X^-+AgNO_3\rightarrow AgX\downarrow+NO^{3-}$

3. **Acidification:**

   - Add nitric acid to the solution to ensure that the medium is sufficiently acidic. This prevents the formation of other silver salts that might interfere with the titration.

4. **Removal of Precipitate:**

   - Filter the solution to remove the precipitated silver halides (AgX). The filtrate contains the excess unreacted silver ions (Ag^+).

5. **Back-Titration with Thiocyanate:**

- Add a few drops of the iron (III) ammonium sulfate indicator to the filtrate. The solution will turn yellow due to the presence of Fe3+ ions.
- Titrate the excess silver ions in the filtrate with the standard ammonium thiocyanate solution. The thiocyanate ions will react with the silver ions to form a white precipitate of silver thiocyanate (AgSCN): $Ag^+ + SCN^- \rightarrow AgSCN\downarrow$
- As the endpoint is approached, add the thiocyanate solution dropwise to avoid overshooting the equivalence point.

6. **Determining the Endpoint:**

- The endpoint is reached when a permanent red color appears, indicating the formation of the red complex between iron(III) ions and excess thiocyanate ions: $Fe^{3+} + 3SCN^- \rightarrow Fe(SCN)_3$
- Record the final volume of the ammonium thiocyanate solution in the burette.

Precautions:

- Ensure all glassware and reagents are clean and free from contaminants.
- Handle silver nitrate and nitric acid with care, as they can be hazardous.
- Perform the titration under consistent lighting conditions to ensure accurate visual comparison.
- Properly dispose of waste according to safety regulations due to the use of hazardous chemicals.

Applications of Modified Volhard's Method:

- Determination of chloride, bromide, and iodide ion concentrations in water samples.
- Analysis of halides in biological fluids and industrial samples.
- Quality control in the pharmaceutical industry for halide content.

6.2 Methods of Precipitation Titrations
6.2.4 Fajans Method

Introduction: Fajans method is a precipitation titration technique that relies on adsorption indicators to determine the endpoint of the titration. This method is particularly useful for the titration of halide ions (such as chloride, bromide, and iodide) with silver nitrate ($AgNO_3$). Unlike other methods that use colorimetric changes in the solution, Fajans method uses indicators that adsorb onto the surface of the precipitate, resulting in a color change that signals the endpoint.

Principle: In Fajans method, an adsorption indicator is used, which adsorbs onto the surface of the precipitate (such as silver halide) at the endpoint. The indicator changes color when it adsorbs onto the positively charged surface of the precipitate, signaling the completion of the titration. The method relies on the formation of a colloidal suspension of the precipitate and the adsorption properties of the indicator.

Reaction Equations:

1. Precipitation of halide ions with silver nitrate: $X^-(aq)+Ag^+(aq)\rightarrow AgX(s)$ (where X- = Cl$^-$, Br$^-$, I$^-$)

Procedure for Fajans Method:

1. **Preparation of Solutions**:

   - **Titrant**: Prepare a standard solution of silver nitrate ($AgNO_3$), typically 0.1 M.
   - **Sample Solution**: Prepare the halide ion solution to be analyzed.
   - **Indicator**: Select an appropriate adsorption indicator, such as fluorescein or eosin.

2. **Indicator Selection**:

   - Choose an adsorption indicator that changes color when adsorbed onto the surface of the precipitate. Common indicators include:

     - **Fluorescein**: Changes from yellow-green to pink.
     - **Eosin**: Changes from pink to red.

3. **Titration Setup**:

- Fill a burette with the standard silver nitrate solution.
- Place the halide ion solution in an Erlenmeyer flask or titration vessel.
- Add a few drops of the selected adsorption indicator to the halide ion solution.

4. Performing the Titration:

- Slowly add the silver nitrate solution from the burette to the halide ion solution while continuously swirling the flask.
- Observe the color change of the indicator. Initially, the solution will not show any significant color change.
- As the titration proceeds, a colloidal suspension of the silver halide precipitate forms.

5. Determining the Endpoint:

- The endpoint is reached when the adsorption indicator changes color due to its adsorption onto the surface of the precipitate. For example, with fluorescein, the color changes from yellow-green to pink.
- Record the final volume of the silver nitrate solution in the burette.

Precautions:

- Ensure all glassware and reagents are clean and free from contaminants.
- Handle silver nitrate with care, as it can stain skin and clothing.
- Perform the titration under consistent lighting conditions to ensure accurate visual comparison.
- Properly dispose of waste according to safety regulations due to the use of hazardous chemicals.

Applications of Fajans Method:

- Determination of chloride, bromide, and iodide ion concentrations in water samples.
- Analysis of halides in pharmaceutical formulations.
- Quality control in various industrial processes involving halide ions.

6.3 Applications

6.3.1 Estimation of Sodium Chloride

Introduction: Sodium chloride (NaCl), commonly known as table salt, is an essential compound widely used in various industries, including food, pharmaceuticals, and chemical manufacturing. Accurate estimation of sodium chloride is crucial for quality control and regulatory compliance. Precipitation titration methods, such as Mohr's method and Volhard's method, are commonly used for the precise determination of sodium chloride concentration in samples.

Principle: The estimation of sodium chloride is based on the precipitation reaction between chloride ions (Cl^-) and silver ions (Ag^+) to form insoluble silver chloride (AgCl). The endpoint of the titration is determined using a suitable indicator that signals the completion of the reaction.

Method 1: Mohr's Method

1. **Preparation of Solutions**:

   - **Titrant**: Prepare a standard solution of silver nitrate ($AgNO_3$), typically 0.1 M.
   - **Sample Solution**: Prepare the sodium chloride solution to be analyzed.
   - **Indicator**: Prepare a 5% potassium chromate (K_2CrO_4) solution.

2. **Indicator Addition**:

   - Add a few drops of the potassium chromate indicator to the sodium chloride solution. The solution will turn yellow due to the chromate ions.

3. **Titration Setup**:

   - Fill a burette with the standard silver nitrate solution.
   - Place the sodium chloride solution in an Erlenmeyer flask or titration vessel.
   - Add the potassium chromate indicator to the sodium chloride solution.

4. **Performing the Titration**:

- Slowly add the silver nitrate solution from the burette to the sodium chloride solution while continuously swirling the flask.
- Observe the color change of the solution. Initially, a white precipitate of silver chloride will form.
- As the endpoint approaches, add the silver nitrate solution dropwise to avoid overshooting the equivalence point.

5. **Determining the Endpoint**:

- The endpoint is reached when a permanent red-brown color appears, indicating the formation of silver chromate (Ag_2CrO_4).
- Record the final volume of the silver nitrate solution in the burette.

Method 2: Volhard's Method

1. **Preparation of Solutions**:

- **Titrant 1**: Prepare a standard solution of silver nitrate ($AgNO_3$), typically 0.1 M.
- **Titrant 2**: Prepare a standard solution of ammonium thiocyanate (NH_4SCN), typically 0.1 M.
- **Sample Solution**: Prepare the sodium chloride solution to be analyzed.
- **Indicator**: Prepare a solution of iron(III) ammonium sulfate (ferric ammonium sulfate).
- **Acid**: Nitric acid (HNO_3) to create an acidic medium.

2. **Precipitation of Chloride Ions**:

- Add a known excess amount of standard silver nitrate solution to the sodium chloride solution. The chloride ions will precipitate as silver chloride: $Cl^- + AgNO_3 \rightarrow AgCl\downarrow + NO_3^-$

3. **Acidification**:

- Add nitric acid to the solution to ensure that the medium is sufficiently acidic. This prevents the formation of other silver salts that might interfere with the titration.

4. **Removal of Precipitate**:

   - Filter the solution to remove the precipitated silver chloride (AgCl). The filtrate contains the excess unreacted silver ions (Ag^+).

5. **Back-Titration with Thiocyanate**:

   - Add a few drops of the iron(III) ammonium sulfate indicator to the filtrate. The solution will turn yellow due to the presence of Fe^{3+} ions.
   - Titrate the excess silver ions in the filtrate with the standard ammonium thiocyanate solution. The thiocyanate ions will react with the silver ions to form a white precipitate of silver thiocyanate (AgSCN): $Ag^+ + SCN^- \rightarrow AgSCN\downarrow$ As the endpoint is approached, add the thiocyanate solution dropwise to avoid overshooting the equivalence point.

6. **Determining the Endpoint**:

   - The endpoint is reached when a permanent red color appears, indicating the formation of the red complex between iron(III) ions and excess thiocyanate ions: $Fe^{3+} + 3SCN^- \rightarrow Fe(SCN)_3$ Record the final volume of the ammonium thiocyanate solution in the burette.

7. **Calculations**:

   - Calculate the total moles of silver nitrate added initially.
   - Calculate the moles of thiocyanate used in the back-titration.
   - The difference between the moles of silver nitrate added and the moles of thiocyanate gives the moles of chloride ions that reacted with the silver ions.
   - Calculate the concentration of sodium chloride using the formula: Concentration of NaCl=Moles of Cl^-×molar mass of NaCl Volume of NaCl solution (L)

SEVEN

COMPLEXOMETRIC TITRATIONS

7.1 Principles of Complexometric Titrations

7.1.1 Complex Formation

Introduction: Complexometric titrations are analytical techniques used to determine the concentration of metal ions in solution by forming stable complexes. These titrations involve the use of complexing agents, known as ligands, which react with metal ions to form soluble complexes. The endpoint of the titration is often detected using metal ion indicators or instrumental methods.

Principle: The principle of complexometric titrations is based on the formation of a stable, soluble complex between a metal ion and a ligand. The stability of these complexes depends on the nature of the metal ion, the ligand, and the conditions of the solution (such as pH). The most common ligand used in complexometric titrations is ethylenediaminetetraacetic acid (EDTA), which can form strong complexes with a wide range of metal ions.

Complex Formation:

1. **Ligands and Metal Ions:**

   - **Ligands** are molecules or ions that can donate electron pairs to a metal ion to form a coordinate covalent bond. Common ligands include EDTA, ammonia, and cyanide.
   - **Metal Ions** are positively charged ions that can accept electron pairs from ligands to form complexes. Examples include calcium (Ca^{2+}), magnesium (Mg^{2+}), and copper (Cu^{2+}).

2. **Stability Constants (Kf):**

   - The stability of a complex is quantified by its formation constant (Kf), also known as the stability constant. A higher Kf indicates a more stable complex.
   - The formation constant is given by the equilibrium expression for the formation of the complex from the metal ion and the ligand.

3. **Example:**

   - Consider the complexation of calcium ions (Ca^{2+}) with EDTA (represented as H4Y in its protonated form):
   - $Ca^{2+} + Y^{4-} \rightleftharpoons CaY^{2-}$ \

4. **Chelation:**

   - Chelation is the process where a single ligand forms multiple coordinate bonds with a metal ion, creating a ring structure. This often leads to more stable complexes.
   - EDTA is a hexadentate ligand, meaning it can form six bonds with a metal ion, creating highly stable chelate complexes.

5. **pH Dependence:**

   - The formation of metal-EDTA complexes is highly pH-dependent. EDTA has four carboxyl groups and two amine groups that can donate electron pairs.
   - At different pH levels, EDTA exists in different protonation states, affecting its ability to complex with metal ions.

Procedure for Complexometric Titration Using EDTA:

1. **Preparation of Solutions:**

   - **Titrant:** Prepare a standard solution of EDTA, typically in the form of disodium EDTA (Na2H2Y).
   - **Sample Solution:** Prepare the metal ion solution to be analyzed.

- **Buffer Solution**: Prepare a buffer solution to maintain the pH at an optimal level for complex formation. Common buffers include ammonia/ammonium chloride for alkaline conditions or acetate buffer for neutral conditions.
- **Indicator**: Select an appropriate metal ion indicator, such as Eriochrome Black T for calcium and magnesium, which changes color when it binds to the metal ion.

2. **Titration Setup**:

- Fill a burette with the standard EDTA solution.
- Place the metal ion solution in an Erlenmeyer flask or titration vessel.
- Add the buffer solution to the metal ion solution to maintain the desired pH.
- Add a few drops of the metal ion indicator to the metal ion solution.

3. **Performing the Titration**:

- Slowly add the EDTA solution from the burette to the metal ion solution while continuously swirling the flask.
- Observe the color change of the indicator. Initially, the solution will have the color of the metal-indicator complex.
- As EDTA is added, it complexes with the free metal ions, displacing the indicator from the metal ions.

4. **Determining the Endpoint**:

- The endpoint is reached when the color of the solution changes, indicating that all the metal ions have been complexed by EDTA, and the indicator is free in solution.
- Record the final volume of the EDTA solution in the burette.

5. **Calculations**:

- Calculate the number of moles of EDTA added using the formula: Moles of EDTA=Molarity of EDTA×Volume of EDTA used (L)
- Since the reaction ratio between the metal ion and EDTA is 1:1, the moles of metal ions in the sample is equal to the moles of EDTA added.

- Calculate the concentration of metal ions using the formula: Concentration of metal ions=Moles of metal ions/ Volume of metal ion solution (L)

7.1 Principles of Complexometric Titrations
7.1.2 Stability Constants

Introduction: The stability constant, also known as the formation constant (Kf), is a crucial parameter in complexometric titrations. It quantifies the stability of a complex ion formed between a metal ion and a ligand. The higher the stability constant, the more stable the complex. Understanding stability constants is essential for predicting the behavior of metal-ligand complexes in solution and for selecting appropriate conditions for titrations.

Principle: The stability constant (Kf) is derived from the equilibrium constant for the formation of a complex ion. For a general reaction where a metal ion (Mn^+) reacts with a ligand (L) to form a complex (MLn):

$$Mn+ +nL \rightleftharpoons MLn$$

The formation constant (Kf) for this reaction is given by:

$$Kf = ([M^{n+}] [L]^n) / [ML^n]$$

Factors Affecting Stability Constants:

1. **Nature of the Metal Ion**:

   - Charge: Higher charge on the metal ion generally increases the stability of the complex.
   - Size: Smaller metal ions form more stable complexes due to stronger electrostatic interactions.
   - Electronic Configuration: Metal ions with a stable electronic configuration tend to form more stable complexes.

2. **Nature of the Ligand**:

   - Denticity: Multidentate ligands (those that can form multiple bonds with the metal ion) generally form more stable complexes than monodentate ligands.
   - Basicity: Ligands with higher basicity (ability to donate electron pairs) tend to form more stable complexes.

- Steric Factors: Ligands that can fit well around the metal ion without causing steric hindrance form more stable complexes.

3. **Environmental Factors**:

- pH: The protonation state of the ligand and the metal ion can affect complex stability. For example, EDTA has different protonation states at different pH levels.
- Solvent: The solvent can influence the stability constant by affecting the solvation of the metal ion and the ligand.

Applications of Stability Constants:

1. **Selection of Ligands**:

- The stability constant helps in selecting ligands for complexometric titrations. Ligands with high stability constants ensure complete complexation of the metal ion.

2. **pH Control**:

- Stability constants are used to determine the optimal pH for the titration. For instance, the formation of metal-EDTA complexes is highly pH-dependent, and the stability constant helps in choosing the appropriate buffer.

3. **Complexometric Indicators**:

- Indicators are selected based on the stability constant of their complexes with metal ions. The indicator should have a lower stability constant than the titrant-metal complex to ensure a clear endpoint.

4. **Environmental Chemistry**:

- Stability constants are used to predict the mobility and bioavailability of metal ions in environmental samples. Stable complexes may reduce the toxicity of heavy metals in water and soil.

7.1 Principles of Complexometric Titrations
7.1.3 Metal Ion Indicators

Introduction: Metal ion indicators are essential in complexometric titrations as they help detect the endpoint by changing color when they form or release a complex with metal ions. These indicators are usually organic compounds that form stable, colored complexes with metal ions. The change in color at the endpoint signifies the completion of the titration.

Principle: The principle behind metal ion indicators is based on their ability to form a colored complex with metal ions in the solution. During the titration, the indicator-metal complex remains stable until the titrant (usually EDTA) is added in sufficient quantity to complex all the metal ions. At the endpoint, the metal ions preferentially complex with the titrant, causing the indicator to release the metal ions and change color, signaling the endpoint of the titration.

Characteristics of Metal Ion Indicators:

1. **Selectivity**: The indicator should selectively bind to the metal ion of interest and form a stable, colored complex.
2. **Distinct Color Change**: The indicator should exhibit a distinct and observable color change at the endpoint to allow for accurate determination.
3. **pH Sensitivity**: The indicator's performance is often pH-dependent, requiring appropriate buffering to maintain the optimal pH during the titration.

Common Metal Ion Indicators:

1. **Eriochrome Black T**:

   - **Color Change**: Red (free indicator) to blue (metal complex).
   - **Optimal pH**: 7-11.
   - **Use**: Commonly used for titrating calcium and magnesium ions.

2. **Calmagite**:

   - **Color Change**: Red (free indicator) to blue (metal complex).
   - **Optimal pH**: 8-10.

- **Use**: Used for titrating calcium and magnesium ions, similar to Eriochrome Black T.

3. **Murexide (Ammonium Purpurate)**:

   - **Color Change**: Yellow (free indicator) to purple (metal complex).
   - **Optimal pH**: 6-12.
   - **Use**: Commonly used for titrating calcium ions.

4. **Xylenol Orange**:

   - **Color Change**: Yellow (free indicator) to red (metal complex).
   - **Optimal pH**: 1.5-3.
   - **Use**: Used for titrating rare earth metals and other metal ions in acidic solutions.

Procedure for Using Metal Ion Indicators in Titrations:

1. **Preparation of Solutions**:

   - **Titrant**: Prepare a standard solution of EDTA.
   - **Sample Solution**: Prepare the metal ion solution to be analyzed.
   - **Buffer Solution**: Prepare a buffer solution to maintain the desired pH.
   - **Indicator Solution**: Prepare a solution of the selected metal ion indicator.

2. **Buffering the Solution**:

   - Add the appropriate buffer to the metal ion solution to maintain the optimal pH for the indicator and the titration.

3. **Addition of Indicator**:

   - Add a few drops of the metal ion indicator to the buffered metal ion solution. Observe the initial color of the solution.

4. **Performing the Titration**:

- ◦ Fill a burette with the standard EDTA solution.
- ◦ Slowly add the EDTA solution from the burette to the metal ion solution while continuously swirling the flask.
- ◦ Monitor the color change of the solution. Initially, the solution will have the color of the metal-indicator complex.

5. **Determining the Endpoint**:

- ◦ The endpoint is reached when the color changes, indicating that all the metal ions have been complexed by EDTA and the indicator is free in solution.
- ◦ Record the final volume of the EDTA solution in the burette.

Applications:

1. **Water Hardness Testing**: Metal ion indicators are used to determine the concentration of calcium and magnesium ions in water, which contribute to water hardness.
2. **Pharmaceutical Analysis**: Used to quantify metal ions in pharmaceutical formulations to ensure proper dosage and stability.
3. **Environmental Analysis**: Applied in the determination of metal ion concentrations in soil and water samples to monitor pollution and contamination levels.
4. **Food and Beverage Industry**: Utilized to measure metal ion content in food and beverage products for quality control and safety compliance.

7.2 Methods and Applications

7.2.1 Masking and Demasking Agents

Introduction: In complexometric titrations, the presence of multiple metal ions can interfere with the accurate determination of the target ion. Masking and demasking agents are used to selectively prevent or allow the reaction of specific metal ions with the titrant. These agents help in achieving accurate and precise measurements by controlling the reactivity of interfering ions.

Principle: Masking agents selectively bind to specific metal ions to form stable, unreactive complexes, effectively "masking" them from participating in the titration. Demasking agents, on the other hand, are used to release the masked ions, making them available for reaction with the titrant. This selective control allows for the sequential determination of different metal ions in the same solution.

Masking Agents:

1. **Cyanide Ion (CN⁻)**:

   - **Function**: Masks ions such as zinc (Zn^{2+}), cadmium (Cd^{2+}), and copper (Cu^{2+}) by forming stable complexes.
   - **Example**: $Zn^{2+}+4CN^-\rightarrow[Zn(CN)4]^{2-}$

2. **Ammonium Fluoride (NH₄F)**:

   - **Function**: Masks iron (III) ions (Fe^{3+}) by forming a stable complex.
   - **Example**: $Fe^{3+}+6F^-\rightarrow[FeF6]^{3-}$

3. **Triethanolamine (TEA)**:

   - **Function**: Masks aluminum (Al^{3+}) and iron (III) ions (Fe^{3+}).
   - **Example**: $Al^{3+}+TEA\rightarrow Al\text{-}TEA$ complex

4. **Tartrate and Citrate Ions**:

   - **Function**: Mask calcium (Ca^{2+}) and magnesium (Mg^{2+}) ions.
   - **Example**: $Ca^{2+}+Tartrate\rightarrow Ca\text{-}Tartrate$ complex
   - **Demasking Agents**:

1. **Formaldehyde**:

   - **Function**: Demasks cyanide complexes by converting cyanide ions into cyanohydrin, releasing the metal ions.
   - **Example**: $[Zn(CN)4]^{2-}+Formaldehyde\rightarrow Zn^{2+}+Cyanohydrin$

2. **Acidic Solutions**:

   - **Function**: Demask fluoride complexes by protonating fluoride ions, releasing the metal ions.
   - **Example**: $[FeF_6]_3^-+6H^+\rightarrow Fe^{3+}+6HF$

3. **Hydrogen Peroxide (H_2O_2):**

  - **Function**: Demasks iron (III) complexes by oxidizing the complexing agent, releasing the metal ions.
  - **Example**: [Fe-TEA complex]+H_2O_2→Fe^{3+}+TEA-oxidized **Procedure for Using Masking and Demasking Agents in Titrations**:

1. **Preparation of Solutions**:

  - **Titrant**: Prepare a standard solution of EDTA.
  - **Sample Solution**: Prepare the metal ion solution to be analyzed.
  - **Buffer Solution**: Prepare a buffer solution to maintain the desired pH.
  - **Indicator Solution**: Prepare a solution of the selected metal ion indicator.
  - **Masking Agent**: Prepare a solution of the appropriate masking agent.

2. **Masking the Interfering Ions**:

  - Add the masking agent to the metal ion solution to selectively mask the interfering ions.
  - Allow sufficient time for the masking reaction to complete, ensuring the interfering ions are effectively masked.

3. **Buffering the Solution**:

  - Add the appropriate buffer to the masked metal ion solution to maintain the optimal pH for the titration.

4. **Addition of Indicator**:

  - Add a few drops of the metal ion indicator to the buffered metal ion solution. Observe the initial color of the solution.

5. **Performing the Titration**:

  - Fill a burette with the standard EDTA solution.
  - Slowly add the EDTA solution from the burette to the masked metal ion solution while continuously swirling the flask.

- Monitor the color change of the solution. Initially, the solution will have the color of the metal-indicator complex.

6. **Determining the Endpoint**:

  - The endpoint is reached when the color changes, indicating that all the target metal ions have been complexed by EDTA and the indicator is free in solution.
  - Record the final volume of the EDTA solution in the burette.

7. **Demasking the Masked Ions** (if required for sequential analysis):

  - Add the demasking agent to the solution to release the previously masked ions.
  - Perform a second titration if sequential determination of another metal ion is required.

Applications:

1. **Water Hardness Testing**: Masking agents are used to selectively mask magnesium ions to determine calcium ions separately.
2. **Pharmaceutical Analysis**: Masking and demasking agents help in the selective determination of metal ions in complex pharmaceutical formulations.
3. **Environmental Analysis**: Used in the analysis of metal ions in soil and water samples, where multiple metal ions may be present.
4. **Food and Beverage Industry**: Applied in the determination of specific metal ions in food and beverage products for quality control and safety compliance.

7.2 Methods and Applications

7.2.2 Estimation of Magnesium Sulphate

Introduction: Magnesium sulphate ($MgSO_4$), commonly known as Epsom salt, is widely used in medicine, agriculture, and various industrial processes. Accurate estimation of magnesium sulphate is essential for quality control and regulatory compliance. Complexometric titration with EDTA is a commonly used method for the precise determination of magnesium ions in magnesium sulphate.

Principle: The estimation of magnesium sulphate is based on the formation of a stable complex between magnesium ions (Mg^{2+}) and EDTA. The endpoint of the titration is detected using an appropriate metal ion indicator that changes color when all the magnesium ions have been complexed by EDTA.

Procedure for Estimation of Magnesium Sulphate:

1. **Preparation of Solutions**:

   - **Titrant**: Prepare a standard solution of EDTA (ethylene diamine tetraacetic acid), typically 0.01 M.
   - **Sample Solution**: Dissolve an accurately weighed amount of magnesium sulphate in distilled water to prepare the sample solution.
   - **Buffer Solution**: Prepare an ammonia/ammonium chloride buffer solution to maintain the pH at around 10.
   - **Indicator**: Use Eriochrome Black T as the indicator, which changes color from wine-red to blue at the endpoint.

2. **Sample Preparation**:

   - Weigh an appropriate amount of magnesium sulphate ($MgSO_4 \cdot 7H2O$) and dissolve it in distilled water to prepare a solution of known concentration.

3. **Titration Setup**:

   - Fill a burette with the standard EDTA solution.
   - Pipette an aliquot (usually 25.0 mL) of the magnesium sulphate solution into a titration flask.
   - Add 5-10 mL of the ammonia/ammonium chloride buffer solution to the flask to maintain the pH at around 10.
   - Add a few drops of Eriochrome Black T indicator to the solution. The solution will turn wine-red due to the formation of the magnesium-indicator complex.

4. **Performing the Titration**:

- Slowly add the EDTA solution from the burette to the magnesium sulphate solution while continuously swirling the flask.
- Observe the color change of the solution. Initially, the solution will remain wine-red.
- As EDTA is added, it complexes with the free magnesium ions, displacing the indicator from the magnesium ions.

5. **Determining the Endpoint**:

- The endpoint is reached when the color changes from wine-red to pure blue, indicating that all the magnesium ions have been complexed by EDTA, and the indicator is free in solution.
- Record the final volume of the EDTA solution in the burette.

Precautions:

- Ensure all glassware and reagents are clean and free from contaminants.
- Handle EDTA and ammonia buffer with care, as they can be hazardous.
- Perform the titration under consistent lighting conditions to ensure accurate visual comparison.
- Properly dispose of waste according to safety regulations due to the use of hazardous chemicals.

Applications:

1. **Pharmaceutical Industry**: Estimation of magnesium sulphate in pharmaceutical formulations to ensure proper dosage and quality.
2. **Agriculture**: Determination of magnesium content in soil and fertilizers for assessing nutrient availability and soil health.
3. **Water Treatment**: Analysis of magnesium levels in water samples to monitor hardness and water quality.
4. **Food and Beverage Industry**: Measurement of magnesium content in food and beverage products for quality control and nutritional labeling.

7.2 Methods and Applications

7.2.3 Estimation of Calcium Gluconate

Introduction: Calcium gluconate is a calcium salt of gluconic acid commonly used as a calcium supplement in medicine. Accurate estimation of calcium gluconate is essential in pharmaceutical quality control to ensure proper dosage and therapeutic efficacy. Complexometric titration with EDTA is a reliable method for the precise determination of calcium ions in calcium gluconate.

Principle: The estimation of calcium gluconate is based on the formation of a stable complex between calcium ions (Ca^{2+}) and EDTA. The endpoint of the titration is detected using a suitable metal ion indicator that changes color when all the calcium ions have been complexed by EDTA.

Procedure for Estimation of Calcium Gluconate:

1. **Preparation of Solutions**:

   - **Titrant**: Prepare a standard solution of EDTA (ethylene diamine tetraacetic acid), typically 0.01 M.
   - **Sample Solution**: Dissolve an accurately weighed amount of calcium gluconate in distilled water to prepare the sample solution.
   - **Buffer Solution**: Prepare an ammonia/ammonium chloride buffer solution to maintain the pH at around 10.
   - **Indicator**: Use Eriochrome Black T as the indicator, which changes color from wine-red to blue at the endpoint.

2. **Sample Preparation**:

   - Weigh an appropriate amount of calcium gluconate and dissolve it in distilled water to prepare a solution of known concentration.

3. **Titration Setup**:

   - Fill a burette with the standard EDTA solution.
   - Pipette an aliquot (usually 25.0 mL) of the calcium gluconate solution into a titration flask.
   - Add 5-10 mL of the ammonia/ammonium chloride buffer solution to the flask to maintain the pH at around 10.
   - Add a few drops of Eriochrome Black T indicator to the solution. The solution will turn wine-red due to the formation of the calcium-indicator complex.

4. **Performing the Titration**:

- Slowly add the EDTA solution from the burette to the calcium gluconate solution while continuously swirling the flask.
- Observe the color change of the solution. Initially, the solution will remain wine-red.
- As EDTA is added, it complexes with the free calcium ions, displacing the indicator from the calcium ions.

5. **Determining the Endpoint**:

- The endpoint is reached when the color changes from wine-red to pure blue, indicating that all the calcium ions have been complexed by EDTA, and the indicator is free in solution.
- Record the final volume of the EDTA solution in the burette.

Precautions:

- Ensure all glassware and reagents are clean and free from contaminants.
- Handle EDTA and ammonia buffer with care, as they can be hazardous.
- Perform the titration under consistent lighting conditions to ensure accurate visual comparison.
- Properly dispose of waste according to safety regulations due to the use of hazardous chemicals.

Applications:

1. **Pharmaceutical Industry**: Estimation of calcium gluconate in pharmaceutical formulations to ensure proper dosage and quality.
2. **Clinical Laboratories**: Measurement of calcium levels in biological samples for diagnostic purposes.
3. **Nutritional Supplements**: Analysis of calcium content in dietary supplements to ensure accurate labeling and dosage.
4. **Food and Beverage Industry**: Determination of calcium content in food and beverage products for quality control and nutritional labeling.

EIGHT

GRAVIMETRIC ANALYSIS

8.1 Principles of Gravimetric Analysis

8.1.1 Precipitation and Filtration

Introduction: Gravimetric analysis is a quantitative chemical analysis method used to determine the amount of an analyte based on the mass of a solid. It involves the transformation of the analyte into an insoluble precipitate, which is then filtered, dried, and weighed. The mass of the precipitate is used to calculate the amount of the analyte.

Principle: The principle of gravimetric analysis is based on the accurate measurement of the mass of a precipitate. The process involves several steps, including precipitation, filtration, washing, drying or igniting, and weighing. The success of gravimetric analysis depends on the formation of a pure, stable, and insoluble precipitate.

Precipitation and Filtration:

1. **Precipitation**:

   - **Formation of Precipitate**: The analyte is converted into an insoluble precipitate by adding a suitable precipitating agent. The choice of the precipitating agent is crucial for forming a pure and easily filterable precipitate.

   - **Saturation**: The solution should be sufficiently concentrated to achieve supersaturation, which is necessary for nucleation and growth of precipitate particles.

- **Supersaturation**: Supersaturation is the condition where the concentration of the dissolved substance exceeds its solubility. It is essential for the nucleation of the precipitate.
- **Nucleation and Particle Growth**: The process of nucleation involves the formation of small, stable particles, which grow into larger particles that can be easily filtered. Controlling the rate of nucleation and particle growth is important to obtain a precipitate with desirable properties.

2. **Factors Affecting Precipitation**:

- **Solubility Product (Ksp)**: The lower the solubility product of the precipitate, the less soluble it is, which aids in complete precipitation.
- **Temperature**: Higher temperatures generally increase solubility, but they also increase the rate of particle growth, which can result in larger and more easily filterable particles.
- **pH**: The pH of the solution can affect the solubility of the precipitate. Proper pH adjustment can enhance the formation of the precipitate.
- **Common Ion Effect**: The presence of a common ion can decrease the solubility of the precipitate, aiding in its formation.

3. **Filtration**:

- **Selection of Filter Medium**: The filter medium should be chosen based on the size and nature of the precipitate particles. Common filter media include filter paper, sintered glass, and membrane filters.
- **Preparation of Filter**: The filter medium should be properly prepared, often by washing with distilled water to remove any impurities.
- **Filtration Process**: The precipitate is separated from the solution by filtration. The solution containing the precipitate is poured through the filter medium, which retains the solid particles while allowing the liquid to pass through.
- **Washing the Precipitate**: The precipitate is washed with a suitable solvent, usually distilled water, to remove any impurities that might be co-precipitated or adsorbed on the surface. Proper washing is crucial to ensure the purity of the precipitate.

Example Procedure for Gravimetric Analysis:

1. **Sample Preparation**:

   - Dissolve the sample in an appropriate solvent to obtain a clear solution.

2. **Precipitation**:

   - Add a suitable precipitating agent to the solution. For example, to precipitate chloride ions as silver chloride, add a solution of silver nitrate ($AgNO_3$): $Cl^-(aq)+Ag^+(aq) \rightarrow AgCl(s)$

3. **Digestion**:

   - Allow the precipitate to stand in the solution (digestion) to promote the growth of larger, purer crystals. This step enhances the filterability and purity of the precipitate.

4. **Filtration**:

   - Set up a filtration apparatus with a pre-weighed filter paper or crucible.
   - Filter the precipitate, ensuring that all the solid is transferred to the filter medium.

5. **Washing**:

   - Wash the precipitate with small portions of distilled water to remove soluble impurities. Repeat this process several times.

6. **Drying or Igniting**:

   - Dry the precipitate to a constant weight by placing it in an oven at a specified temperature. Alternatively, if the precipitate requires ignition, place it in a crucible and heat in a muffle furnace to convert it to a stable form.

7. **Weighing**:

- Allow the dried or ignited precipitate to cool in a desiccator to prevent moisture absorption.
- Weigh the cooled precipitate using an analytical balance to obtain the mass of the precipitate.

8. **Calculations**:

- Use the mass of the precipitate to calculate the amount of the analyte based on the stoichiometry of the precipitation reaction.
- For example, in the case of chloride ion determination using silver nitrate: Mass of AgCl→Moles of AgCl→Moles of Cl-→Mass of Cl-

Example Calculation:

1. **Titration Data**:

- Mass of filter paper: 1.000 g
- Mass of filter paper + dried AgCl: 1.245 g
- Mass of AgCl: 1.245 g - 1.000 g = 0.245 g

2. **Calculations**:

- Molar mass of AgCl = 143.32 g/mol
- Moles of AgCl: Moles of AgCl=0.245 g / 143.32 g/mol=0.00171 moles Moles of Cl- (1:1 molar ratio):
- Moles of Cl-=0.00171 moles
- Mass of Cl- =0.00171 moles×35.45 g/mol=0.0607 g

8.1 Principles of Gravimetric Analysis
8.1.2 Drying and Weighing
Introduction: Drying and weighing are critical steps in gravimetric analysis that ensure the accuracy and precision of the final results. After precipitation and filtration, the precipitate must be free from any adhering solvent and volatile impurities. Drying (or ignition) removes these, ensuring that only the mass of the desired compound is measured.

Principle: The principle behind drying and weighing is to obtain a stable, constant mass for the precipitate. This mass is used to calculate the amount of the analyte in the original sample. Proper drying ensures that no moisture or other volatiles remain, which could otherwise lead to errors in the final mass measurement.

Drying:

1. **Purpose:**

   - Remove moisture and volatile impurities.
   - Ensure the precipitate is in a stable form for accurate weighing.

2. **Methods of Drying:**

   - **Oven Drying:** Commonly used for many precipitates. The precipitate is dried in an oven at a specific temperature (typically 100-110°C) until a constant weight is achieved.
   - **Air Drying:** Used for heat-sensitive precipitates. The precipitate is allowed to dry in air or in a desiccator.
   - **Desiccator Drying:** Involves placing the precipitate in a desiccator over a desiccant (e.g., silica gel) to remove moisture without heat.
   - **Ignition:** For precipitates that need to be converted to a stable form, the precipitate is heated in a muffle furnace at high temperatures (e.g., 500-1000°C).

3. **Steps for Drying:**

   - Place the filtered precipitate (with filter paper or in a crucible) in the drying apparatus.
   - For oven drying, set the temperature and dry the sample for a specified period.
   - For ignition, place the crucible in a muffle furnace and heat to the required temperature.
   - Allow the precipitate to cool to room temperature, preferably in a desiccator to avoid moisture uptake from the air.

Weighing:

1. **Purpose:**

- Accurately measure the mass of the dried precipitate to determine the amount of analyte.

2. **Equipment**:

- **Analytical Balance**: Highly precise balance used to measure the mass of the dried precipitate to at least four decimal places.
- **Desiccator**: Used to cool the precipitate after drying and to keep it free from moisture before weighing.

3. **Steps for Weighing**:

- Ensure the analytical balance is calibrated and clean.
- Transfer the dried precipitate (or the crucible containing the precipitate) to a desiccator and allow it to cool to room temperature.
- Weigh the empty crucible or filter paper (tare weight) and record the mass.
- Weigh the crucible or filter paper with the dried precipitate and record the mass.
- Calculate the mass of the precipitate by subtracting the tare weight from the total weight.

Example Procedure for Drying and Weighing:

1. **Sample Preparation**:

- Precipitate the analyte from the solution and filter it onto pre-weighed filter paper or into a crucible.

2. **Drying**:

- Place the filter paper or crucible with the precipitate in an oven set to 105°C.
- Dry the sample for several hours or until a constant weight is achieved.
- Alternatively, place the crucible in a muffle furnace and ignite at 800°C if the precipitate requires conversion to a stable form.

3. **Cooling**:

- Transfer the dried or ignited precipitate to a desiccator and allow it to cool to room temperature.

4. **Weighing**:

- Weigh the cooled filter paper or crucible on an analytical balance.
- Record the mass of the dried precipitate along with the tare weight of the filter paper or crucible.

8.2 Purity of the Precipitate
8.2.1 Co-precipitation

Introduction: Co-precipitation is a phenomenon that occurs during the precipitation process where impurities are incorporated into the precipitate along with the desired analyte. This can significantly affect the accuracy and purity of the results in gravimetric analysis. Understanding the mechanisms of co-precipitation and how to minimize its effects is crucial for obtaining precise and accurate measurements.

Principle: Co-precipitation involves the unintended inclusion of foreign ions or compounds within the precipitate. This can occur through several mechanisms, including surface adsorption, occlusion, and inclusion. Each mechanism can introduce different types of impurities into the precipitate, thereby affecting its purity and the accuracy of the analytical results.

Mechanisms of Co-precipitation:

1. **Surface Adsorption**:

- **Description**: Surface adsorption occurs when impurities adhere to the surface of the precipitate particles.
- **Example**: During the precipitation of silver chloride (AgCl), foreign ions like sodium (Na+) or potassium (K+) can adsorb onto the surface of the AgCl particles.
- **Mitigation**: Repeated washing of the precipitate with distilled water can help remove surface-adsorbed impurities.

2. **Occlusion**:

- **Description**: Occlusion happens when impurities are trapped within the crystal lattice of the precipitate as it forms.
- **Example**: If a solution containing calcium ions (Ca2+) is precipitated as calcium oxalate (CaC2O4), impurities like magnesium ions (Mg2+) can get occluded within the crystal lattice.
- **Mitigation**: Slow precipitation and digestion (allowing the precipitate to sit in the mother liquor) can reduce occlusion by promoting the growth of purer, larger crystals.

3. Inclusion:

- **Description**: Inclusion occurs when foreign ions of similar size and charge to the analyte ions are incorporated into the crystal structure of the precipitate.
- **Example**: In the precipitation of barium sulfate (BaSO4), strontium ions (Sr2+), which have a similar ionic radius to barium ions (Ba2+), can be included in the crystal structure.
- **Mitigation**: Adjusting the ionic strength and controlling the precipitation conditions can help minimize inclusion.

Example Procedure for Minimizing Co-precipitation:

1. Sample Preparation:

- Dissolve the sample in an appropriate solvent to obtain a clear solution.

2. Precipitation:

- Add the precipitating agent slowly to the solution while stirring continuously. This helps in the formation of larger and purer crystals.
- Example: For the precipitation of silver chloride, slowly add silver nitrate (AgNO3) to a solution containing chloride ions.

3. Digestion:

- Allow the precipitate to stand in the mother liquor for an extended period (usually a few hours). Digestion helps in the recrystallization process, which can expel occluded impurities and form larger, purer crystals.

4. **Filtration:**

   - Filter the precipitate using a suitable filter medium. Ensure that the filtration is done efficiently to avoid loss of the precipitate.

5. **Washing:**

   - Wash the precipitate thoroughly with distilled water or an appropriate solvent to remove surface-adsorbed impurities. Several washings might be necessary to ensure purity.
   - Example: For washing silver chloride, use cold distilled water to minimize solubility losses.

6. **Drying or Igniting:**

   - Dry the precipitate in an oven at the specified temperature or ignite it in a muffle furnace if required.
   - Allow the precipitate to cool in a desiccator before weighing.

7. **Weighing:**

   - Weigh the dried or ignited precipitate accurately using an analytical balance.

Example Calculation for Co-precipitation:

1. **Titration Data:**

   - Mass of crucible: 25.000 g
   - Mass of crucible + dried precipitate: 25.500 g
   - Mass of precipitate: 0.500 g

2. **Calculations:**

- If the precipitate is suspected to contain impurities, perform qualitative analysis on the washings to identify and quantify the impurities.
- Calculate the corrected mass of the precipitate by subtracting the mass of the identified impurities.

8.2 Purity of the Precipitate
8.2.2 Post-precipitation

Introduction: Post-precipitation occurs when a second, less soluble compound precipitates onto an already formed precipitate during the filtration or washing stages. This can lead to contamination and inaccurate results in gravimetric analysis. Understanding post-precipitation and how to minimize its effects is crucial for ensuring the purity and accuracy of the final precipitate.

Principle: Post-precipitation involves the formation of an unwanted precipitate that co-deposits with the desired analyte after the primary precipitation process has occurred. This typically happens during the standing period after the initial precipitation and before filtration, or during the washing of the precipitate. Proper control of the experimental conditions can minimize post-precipitation.

Mechanisms of Post-precipitation:

1. **Sequential Precipitation:**

   - **Description**: Different compounds precipitate at different rates and under varying conditions. Post-precipitation occurs when a second compound starts to precipitate after the primary precipitation is complete.
   - **Example**: In the precipitation of calcium oxalate (CaC_2O_4), if the solution contains iron (III) ions, ferric hydroxide ($Fe(OH)_3$) may precipitate post-precipitation if the solution pH changes.

2. **Super-Saturation:**

   - **Description**: If the solution becomes supersaturated with respect to a secondary compound after the initial precipitate is formed, the secondary compound can begin to precipitate.

- **Example**: After the precipitation of barium sulfate ($BaSO_4$), if sulfate concentration increases due to evaporation or temperature changes, additional sulfate salts may precipitate.

3. **Inadvertent Contamination**:

  - **Description**: Contamination can occur from reagents, glassware, or the environment, leading to post-precipitation of unintended compounds.
  - **Example**: Contaminants from washing solutions can cause post-precipitation of foreign ions onto the primary precipitate.

Strategies to Minimize Post-precipitation:

1. **Control of Conditions**:

  - **Temperature**: Maintain a consistent temperature to avoid changes in solubility that can lead to post-precipitation.
  - **pH**: Carefully control the pH of the solution to prevent the formation of additional precipitates.

2. **Rapid Filtration**:

  - Filter the precipitate as soon as possible after formation to minimize the time available for post-precipitation to occur.

3. **Use of Pure Reagents**:

  - Ensure all reagents and solvents are pure and free from contaminants that could cause post-precipitation.

4. **Thorough Washing**:

  - Wash the precipitate thoroughly with an appropriate solvent to remove any ions that could cause post-precipitation.

Example Procedure for Minimizing Post-precipitation:

1. **Sample Preparation:**

   ○ Dissolve the sample in an appropriate solvent to obtain a clear solution.

2. **Precipitation:**

   ○ Add the precipitating agent to the solution while maintaining controlled conditions (e.g., temperature and pH) to form the primary precipitate.
   ○ Example: For the precipitation of calcium oxalate, add oxalic acid to the solution containing calcium ions while maintaining a slightly acidic pH.

3. **Filtration:**

   ○ Rapidly filter the precipitate to minimize the opportunity for post-precipitation. Use a pre-weighed filter paper or crucible for filtration.

4. **Washing:**

   ○ Wash the precipitate with a small volume of cold distilled water to remove soluble impurities.
   ○ Use a wash solution that does not cause the precipitation of additional compounds.

5. **Drying or Igniting:**

   ○ Dry the precipitate in an oven at the specified temperature or ignite it in a muffle furnace if required.
   ○ Allow the precipitate to cool in a desiccator before weighing.

6. **Weighing:**

   ○ Weigh the dried or ignited precipitate accurately using an analytical balance.

Example Calculation for Post-precipitation:

1. **Titration Data**:

   - Mass of crucible: 25.000 g
   - Mass of crucible + dried precipitate: 25.500 g
   - Mass of precipitate: 0.500 g

2. **Qualitative Analysis**:

   - If post-precipitation is suspected, perform qualitative analysis on the washings to identify and quantify any additional precipitates.

3. **Calculations**:

   - Calculate the corrected mass of the primary precipitate by subtracting the mass of the post-precipitated compounds, if identified and quantified.

   8.2 Purity of the Precipitate
   8.2.3 Methods to Ensure Purity
   Introduction: Ensuring the purity of the precipitate is crucial in gravimetric analysis to obtain accurate and reliable results. Impurities in the precipitate can arise from various sources, including co-precipitation, post-precipitation, and contamination. Implementing effective methods to ensure the purity of the precipitate enhances the precision and accuracy of the analytical process.
   Methods to Ensure Purity:

1. **Selection of Suitable Precipitating Agent**:

   - Choose a precipitating agent that forms a stable, insoluble compound with the analyte. The precipitate should have low solubility in the solution to minimize losses.
   - Example: Use barium chloride ($BaCl_2$) for precipitating sulfate ions (SO_4^{2-}) as barium sulfate ($BaSO_4$), which is highly insoluble.

2. **Optimal Precipitation Conditions**:

- ○ Control the pH: Adjust the pH of the solution to ensure maximum precipitation of the desired compound while minimizing the precipitation of impurities.

    - ▪ Example: Precipitating calcium as calcium oxalate (CaC_2O_4) requires a slightly acidic to neutral pH to prevent the precipitation of magnesium oxalate.

- ○ Control the Temperature: Maintain a consistent temperature to avoid changes in solubility that can lead to the precipitation of unwanted compounds.
- ○ Control the Rate of Precipitation: Add the precipitating agent slowly and with constant stirring to promote the formation of larger, purer crystals. Rapid addition can lead to the inclusion of impurities.

3. Digestion:

- ○ Allow the precipitate to stand in the mother liquor (the solution from which the precipitate forms) for an extended period. Digestion helps in the growth of larger and purer crystals by dissolving smaller, impure particles and reprecipitating them on larger crystals.
- ○ Example: Allowing the precipitate of silver chloride (AgCl) to digest can help expel occluded impurities and form larger, purer crystals.

4. Thorough Washing:

- ○ Wash the precipitate with a suitable solvent (usually cold distilled water) to remove soluble impurities. The washing should be thorough but gentle to avoid loss of the precipitate.
- ○ Use a wash solution that does not dissolve the precipitate or cause the precipitation of additional compounds.
- ○ Example: Washing barium sulfate ($BaSO_4$) with cold distilled water removes soluble impurities without dissolving the $BaSO_4$ precipitate.

5. Reprecipitation:

- ○ Dissolve the initial precipitate in a suitable solvent and reprecipitate it to further purify the compound. This step can help remove co-precipitated impurities.

- ○ Example: Dissolving and reprecipitating calcium oxalate (CaC_2O_4) can help achieve a higher purity of the final precipitate.

6. **Avoiding Contamination**:

- ○ Use clean glassware and high-purity reagents to prevent contamination.
- ○ Avoid contact with dust and other environmental contaminants by covering the precipitation vessel when not in use.

7. **Post-precipitation Control**:

- ○ Minimize the time between precipitation and filtration to reduce the risk of post-precipitation.
- ○ Filter the precipitate as soon as possible after formation and wash it immediately to remove any adhering impurities.

Example Procedure for Ensuring Purity:

1. **Sample Preparation**:

- ○ Dissolve the sample in an appropriate solvent to obtain a clear solution.

2. **Precipitation**:

- ○ Add the precipitating agent slowly while stirring continuously. For example, add silver nitrate ($AgNO_3$) to a solution containing chloride ions to precipitate silver chloride ($AgCl$).

3. **Digestion**:

- ○ Allow the precipitate to stand in the mother liquor for a specified period (e.g., several hours) to promote the growth of larger, purer crystals.

4. **Filtration**:

- Filter the precipitate using pre-weighed filter paper or a crucible. Ensure efficient filtration to avoid loss of the precipitate.

5. **Washing**:

- Wash the precipitate with small portions of cold distilled water to remove soluble impurities. Repeat the washing process several times.

6. **Reprecipitation (if necessary)**:

- Dissolve the initial precipitate in a suitable solvent and reprecipitate it by adding the precipitating agent again.

7. **Drying or Igniting**:

- Dry the precipitate in an oven at the specified temperature or ignite it in a muffle furnace if required.
- Allow the precipitate to cool in a desiccator before weighing.

8. **Weighing**:

- Weigh the dried or ignited precipitate accurately using an analytical balance.

Example Calculation for Purity:

1. **Titration Data**:

- Mass of crucible: 25.000 g
- Mass of crucible + dried precipitate: 25.500 g
- Mass of precipitate: 0.500 g

2. **Qualitative Analysis**:

- Perform qualitative analysis on the washings to identify and quantify any remaining impurities.

3. **Calculations**:

- If impurities are identified, subtract their mass from the total mass of the precipitate to obtain the corrected mass of the pure analyte.

8.3 Applications

8.3.1 Estimation of Barium Sulphate

Introduction: Barium sulphate ($BaSO_4$) is a white crystalline solid that is widely used in various industries, including medicine, oil and gas drilling, and manufacturing. In gravimetric analysis, the estimation of barium as barium sulphate is a common method for determining the sulfate content in a sample. This method relies on the precipitation of sulfate ions with barium ions to form insoluble barium sulphate, which is then filtered, dried, and weighed.

Principle: The estimation of barium sulphate is based on the precipitation reaction between barium ions (Ba^{2+}) and sulfate ions (SO_4^{2-}) to form insoluble barium sulphate ($BaSO4$). The precipitate is collected by filtration, washed, dried, and weighed. The mass of the barium sulphate precipitate is used to calculate the amount of sulfate in the original sample.

Chemical Reaction: $Ba^{2+}(aq) + SO_4^{2-}(aq) \rightarrow BaSO_4(s)$

Procedure for Estimation of Barium Sulphate:

1. **Preparation of Solutions**:

   - **Sample Solution**: Dissolve the sample containing sulfate ions in distilled water to prepare a clear solution.
   - **Precipitating Agent**: Prepare a 0.1 M solution of barium chloride ($BaCl_2$).

2. **Precipitation**:

   - Heat the sample solution to near boiling to ensure complete reaction and to improve the filterability of the precipitate.
   - Slowly add the barium chloride solution to the hot sample solution while continuously stirring. The sulfate ions in the sample will react with the barium ions to form barium sulphate precipitate.
   - Continue adding barium chloride until no more precipitate forms, indicating complete precipitation of sulfate ions.

3. **Digestion**:

- Allow the precipitate to digest by standing in the hot solution for about 30 minutes. Digestion helps to form larger and purer crystals of barium sulphate.

4. **Filtration**:

- Set up a filtration apparatus with pre-weighed filter paper or a crucible.
- Filter the hot solution to collect the barium sulphate precipitate. Use a vacuum filtration system if available to speed up the process.

5. **Washing**:

- Wash the precipitate with small portions of hot distilled water to remove any soluble impurities, particularly chloride ions. Repeat the washing process several times.

6. **Drying**:

- Dry the filtered barium sulphate precipitate in an oven at 105°C until a constant weight is achieved.
- Alternatively, if the precipitate needs to be ignited, place the crucible in a muffle furnace and heat to 800°C to ensure complete drying and to convert the precipitate to a stable form.

7. **Weighing**:

- Allow the dried or ignited precipitate to cool in a desiccator to prevent moisture absorption.
- Weigh the cooled precipitate using an analytical balance.

Precautions:

- Ensure all glassware and reagents are clean and free from contaminants.
- Handle barium chloride with care, as it is toxic.
- Perform the precipitation at near-boiling temperatures to ensure complete reaction and better filterability.
- Thoroughly wash the precipitate to remove soluble impurities.

- Use a desiccator to cool the precipitate before weighing to avoid moisture uptake.

Applications:

1. **Environmental Analysis**: Estimation of sulfate content in water and soil samples to monitor pollution and environmental health.
2. **Pharmaceutical Industry**: Determination of sulfate impurities in pharmaceutical products to ensure compliance with quality standards.
3. **Industrial Processes**: Analysis of sulfate content in raw materials and products in industries such as chemicals, fertilizers, and textiles.
4. **Oil and Gas**: Monitoring sulfate levels in drilling fluids and produced water to prevent scaling and corrosion in pipelines and equipment.

NINE
REDOX TITRATIONS

Introduction to Redox Titrations

Redox titrations are a type of volumetric analysis where the reaction involves the transfer of electrons between the analyte and the titrant. These titrations are used to determine the concentration of an oxidizing or reducing agent in a solution. The endpoint of the titration is detected through various methods, such as color change, use of redox indicators, or potentiometric measurements.

Principle of Redox Titrations

The principle of redox titrations is based on the redox reactions, where oxidation and reduction occur simultaneously. An oxidizing agent gains electrons (is reduced), while a reducing agent loses electrons (is oxidized). The point at which the reaction is complete is called the equivalence point, which can be determined using an appropriate indicator or an electrode that measures the potential change in the solution.

Common Types of Redox Titrations

1. **Permanganometry:**

   - **Titrant:** Potassium permanganate ($KMnO_4$) acts as a strong oxidizing agent.
   - **Indicator:** $KMnO_4$ itself acts as its own indicator, as it imparts a pink or purple color to the solution.

2. **Iodometry:**

- **Titrant**: Iodine (I_2) is used as the titrant, which acts as an oxidizing agent.
- **Indicator**: Starch is used as an indicator, which forms a blue-black complex with iodine.

3. **Cerimetry**:

   - **Titrant**: Cerium(IV) sulfate ($Ce(SO_4)_2$) acts as a strong oxidizing agent.
   - **Indicator**: Ferroin or N-phenylanthranilic acid can be used as an indicator.

4. **Bromatometry**:

   - **Titrant**: Bromine (Br_2) is used as the titrant.
   - **Indicator**: Phenolphthalein or methyl orange can be used as indicators.

5. **Dichrometry**:

   - **Titrant**: Potassium dichromate ($K_2Cr_2O_7$) acts as an oxidizing agent.
   - **Indicator**: Diphenylamine or barium diphenylaminesulfonate can be used as indicators.

Applications of Redox Titrations

Redox titrations are widely used in various fields, including:

- **Pharmaceutical Analysis**: Determining the purity and concentration of pharmaceutical substances.
- **Environmental Analysis**: Measuring the concentration of pollutants and contaminants in water and soil samples.
- **Food Industry**: Assessing the quality and stability of food products by measuring oxidizing or reducing agents.
- **Industrial Chemistry**: Monitoring the concentration of reactants and products in chemical manufacturing processes.

Advantages of Redox Titrations

- **High Precision and Accuracy**: Redox titrations provide precise and accurate results when performed correctly.
- **Wide Range of Applications**: Applicable to various types of samples, including solids, liquids, and gases.
- **Simple and Cost-Effective**: Requires relatively simple equipment and reagents.

Limitations of Redox Titrations

- **Interference**: Presence of other oxidizing or reducing agents in the sample can interfere with the results.
- **Indicator Dependence**: Accurate detection of the endpoint depends on the proper choice of indicator.
- **Environmental Sensitivity**: Redox reactions can be sensitive to changes in temperature and pH, affecting the titration results.

9.1 Concepts of Oxidation and Reduction
9.1.1 Oxidation States

Introduction: Understanding oxidation and reduction (redox) reactions is fundamental in analytical chemistry. These reactions involve the transfer of electrons between chemical species, which can be tracked using oxidation states. The concept of oxidation states helps in identifying which species are oxidized and which are reduced in a chemical reaction.

Principle: The oxidation state (or oxidation number) of an element in a compound is a measure of the degree of oxidation of that element. It is defined as the hypothetical charge that an atom would have if all bonds to atoms of different elements were completely ionic. Oxidation states are used to keep track of electron transfer in redox reactions.

Rules for Assigning Oxidation States:

1. **Pure Elements**: The oxidation state of a pure element is always zero. For example, the oxidation state of O_2, N_2, H_2, and S_8(*an allotrope of sulfur*) is zero.
2. **Monatomic Ions**: The oxidation state of a monatomic ion is equal to its charge. For example, the oxidation state of Na^+ is +1, and the oxidation state of Cl^- is -1.
3. **Oxygen**: In most compounds, oxygen has an oxidation state of -2. Exceptions include peroxides (e.g., H_2O_2), where oxygen has an oxidation

state of -1, and in compounds with fluorine, where it can be positive.

4. **Hydrogen**: In most compounds, hydrogen has an oxidation state of +1. However, in metal hydrides (e.g., NaH), hydrogen has an oxidation state of -1.

5. **Fluorine**: Fluorine always has an oxidation state of -1 in its compounds because it is the most electronegative element.

6. **Sum of Oxidation States**: The sum of the oxidation states of all atoms in a neutral compound must be zero. In a polyatomic ion, the sum of the oxidation states must equal the charge of the ion.

7. **Other Halogens**: Other halogens (Cl, Br, I) typically have an oxidation state of -1 unless they are combined with oxygen or other halogens.

Examples and Application:

1. **Water (H_2O):**

   - Oxidation state of hydrogen (H): +1
   - Oxidation state of oxygen (O): -2
   - Sum of oxidation states: $(2 \times +1) + (-2) = 0$

2. **Hydrogen Peroxide (H_2O_2):**

   - Oxidation state of hydrogen (H): +1
   - Oxidation state of oxygen (O): -1
   - Sum of oxidation states: $(2 \times +1) + (2 \times -1) = 0$

3. **Sodium Chloride (NaCl):**

   - Oxidation state of sodium (Na): +1
   - Oxidation state of chlorine (Cl): -1
   - Sum of oxidation states: $+1 + (-1) = 0$

4. **Sulfuric Acid (H_2SO_4):**

   - Oxidation state of hydrogen (H): +1
   - Oxidation state of oxygen (O): -2
   - Let the oxidation state of sulfur (S) be x.
   - Sum of oxidation states: $(2 \times +1) + x + (4 \times -2) = 0$

- $2 + x - 8 = 0$
- $x = +6$
- Oxidation state of sulfur (S) is +6.

Balancing Redox Reactions:

1. **Identify Oxidation and Reduction Half-Reactions:**

   - Separate the overall redox reaction into two half-reactions: one for oxidation and one for reduction.

2. **Balance Atoms Other Than O and H:**

   - Balance the atoms in each half-reaction, except for oxygen and hydrogen.

3. **Balance Oxygen Atoms:**

   - Add water (H_2O) molecules to balance the oxygen atoms.

4. **Balance Hydrogen Atoms:**

   - Add hydrogen ions ($H+$) to balance the hydrogen atoms.

5. **Balance Charges:**

   - Add electrons (e-) to one side of each half-reaction to balance the charges.

6. **Combine Half-Reactions:**

   - Multiply each half-reaction by an appropriate factor so that the number of electrons gained in the reduction half-reaction equals the number of electrons lost in the oxidation half-reaction.
   - Add the two half-reactions together and cancel out any common species.

Example of Balancing a Redox Reaction:

Unbalanced Reaction: $MnO4^- + Fe^{2+} \rightarrow Mn^{2+} + Fe^{3+}$

Oxidation Half-Reaction (Iron is oxidized): $Fe^{2+} \rightarrow Fe^{3+} + e^-$

Reduction Half-Reaction (Manganese is reduced): $MnO4^- + 8 H^+ + 5e^- \rightarrow Mn^{2+} + 4 H_2O$

Balance Electrons:

- Multiply the oxidation half-reaction by 5 to balance the electrons: $5\,Fe^{2+} \rightarrow 5Fe^{3+} + 5e^-$
- **Combine Half-Reactions**: $5Fe^{2+} + MnO_4^- + 8H^+ \rightarrow 5Fe^{3+} + Mn^{2+} + 4H_2O$
- **9.1 Concepts of Oxidation and Reduction**

9.1.2 Redox Reactions

Introduction: Redox reactions, short for reduction-oxidation reactions, are chemical processes in which the oxidation states of atoms are changed. These reactions involve the transfer of electrons between substances. One substance undergoes oxidation (loses electrons), while the other undergoes reduction (gains electrons). Redox reactions are essential in various chemical processes, including metabolism, combustion, and industrial applications.

Principle: The principle of redox reactions is based on the transfer of electrons between chemical species. The substance that loses electrons is said to be oxidized, while the substance that gains electrons is said to be reduced. The electron transfer can be tracked using oxidation states, which help identify the oxidizing and reducing agents in the reaction.

Definitions:

- **Oxidation**: The process of losing electrons, resulting in an increase in oxidation state.
- **Reduction**: The process of gaining electrons, resulting in a decrease in oxidation state.
- **Oxidizing Agent**: The substance that accepts electrons and is reduced.
- **Reducing Agent**: The substance that donates electrons and is oxidized.

Examples of Redox Reactions:

1. **Combustion of Methane**: $CH_4 + 2O_2 \rightarrow CO_2 + 2H_2O$

   - **Oxidation Half-Reaction**: $CH_4 \rightarrow CO_2 + 8H^+ + 8e^-$

- ○ **Reduction Half-Reaction**: $2O_2+8e-\rightarrow 4O_2^{-2}$
- ○ **Overall Reaction**: $CH_4+2O_2\rightarrow CO_2+2H_2O$

2. **Electrolysis of Water**: $2H_2O\rightarrow 2H_2+O_2$

- ○ **Oxidation Half-Reaction** (at anode): $2H_2O\rightarrow O_2+4H^+ +4e-$
- ○ **Reduction Half-Reaction** (at cathode): $4H^++4e-\rightarrow 2H_2$
- ○ **Overall Reaction**: $2H_2O\rightarrow 2H_2+O_2$

3. **Displacement Reaction**: $Zn+CuSO_4\rightarrow ZnSO_4+Cu$

- ○ **Oxidation Half-Reaction**: $Zn\rightarrow Zn^{2+}+2e-$
- ○ **Reduction Half-Reaction**: $Cu^{2+} +2e-\rightarrow Cu$
- ○ **Overall Reaction**: $Zn+Cu^{2+}\rightarrow Zn^{2+} +Cu$

Balancing Redox Reactions:

1. **Identify the Oxidation and Reduction Half-Reactions:**

- ○ Separate the overall redox reaction into two half-reactions: one for oxidation and one for reduction.

2. **Balance Atoms Other Than Oxygen and Hydrogen:**

- ○ Balance the atoms in each half-reaction, except for oxygen and hydrogen.

3. **Balance Oxygen Atoms:**

- ○ Add water (H_2O) molecules to balance the oxygen atoms in each half-reaction.

4. **Balance Hydrogen Atoms:**

- ○ Add hydrogen ions (H^+) to balance the hydrogen atoms in each half-reaction.

5. **Balance Charges:**

- Add electrons (e-) to one side of each half-reaction to balance the charges.

6. **Combine Half-Reactions**:

   - Multiply each half-reaction by an appropriate factor so that the number of electrons gained in the reduction half-reaction equals the number of electrons lost in the oxidation half-reaction.
   - Add the two half-reactions together and cancel out any common species.

   Example of Balancing a Redox Reaction:
   Unbalanced Reaction: $MnO4- + Fe^{2+} \rightarrow Mn^{2+} + Fe^{3+}$
   Oxidation Half-Reaction (Iron is oxidized): $Fe^{2+} \rightarrow Fe^{3+} + e-$
   Reduction Half-Reaction (Manganese is reduced): $MnO4^- + 8H^+ + 5e- \rightarrow Mn^{2+} + 4H_2O$
   Balance Electrons:

- Multiply the oxidation half-reaction by 5 to balance the electrons: $5Fe^{2+} \rightarrow 5Fe^{3+} + 5e-$ **Combine Half-Reactions**: $5Fe^{2+} + MnO4^- + 8H^+ \rightarrow 5Fe^{3+} + Mn^{2+} + 4H_2O$
- **Applications of Redox Reactions**:

1. **Industrial Processes**:

   - Extraction of metals from ores (e.g., iron extraction in a blast furnace).
   - Production of chemicals such as chlorine, hydrogen, and sodium hydroxide through electrolysis.

2. **Biological Systems**:

   - Cellular respiration and photosynthesis involve redox reactions to produce energy.
   - Enzyme-catalyzed redox reactions are crucial in metabolism.

3. **Environmental Chemistry**:

   - Treatment of wastewater through oxidation-reduction processes.

- Redox reactions in natural water bodies affecting the cycling of nutrients and contaminants.

4. **Analytical Chemistry**:

- Redox titrations for determining the concentration of oxidizing and reducing agents.
- Electrochemical methods like voltammetry and potentiometry rely on redox reactions.

9.1 Concepts of Oxidation and Reduction
9.1.3 Redox Potentials

Introduction: Redox potentials, also known as reduction potentials or oxidation-reduction potentials, are a measure of the tendency of a chemical species to acquire electrons and thereby be reduced. Redox potentials are expressed in volts (V) and are measured relative to a standard reference electrode. Understanding redox potentials is crucial for predicting the direction of redox reactions and for designing electrochemical cells and processes.

Principle: Redox potentials provide a quantitative measure of the driving force behind redox reactions. A higher (more positive) redox potential indicates a greater tendency to gain electrons and be reduced, while a lower (more negative) redox potential indicates a greater tendency to lose electrons and be oxidized. Redox potentials are used to compare the relative strengths of oxidizing and reducing agents.

Standard Reduction Potentials ($E°$):

- Standard reduction potentials are measured under standard conditions: 25°C, 1 M concentration for solutions, 1 atm pressure for gases, and pure solids or liquids.
- The standard hydrogen electrode (SHE) is used as the reference electrode, with a defined potential of 0.00 V.

Using Redox Potentials to Predict Reaction Direction:

- The redox potential of a half-reaction can be used to predict whether a redox reaction will occur spontaneously.

- A redox reaction is spontaneous if the overall cell potential (Ecell) is positive.

Applications of Redox Potentials:

1. **Electrochemical Cells**:

   - Redox potentials are used to design batteries and fuel cells. For instance, in a galvanic cell, a positive cell potential indicates the cell can generate electrical energy spontaneously.

2. **Corrosion Prevention**:

   - Understanding redox potentials helps in designing methods to prevent corrosion, such as galvanization and cathodic protection.

3. **Water Treatment**:

   - Redox potentials are used to monitor and control the oxidation states of contaminants in water treatment processes, ensuring the removal of harmful substances.

4. **Analytical Chemistry**:

   - Redox titrations and potentiometric methods rely on redox potentials to determine the concentration of oxidizing and reducing agents in a sample.

5. **Biochemistry**:

   - Redox potentials are crucial in understanding biochemical processes such as cellular respiration and photosynthesis, where electron transfer is fundamental.

9.2 Types of Redox Titrations
9.2.1 Cerimetry
Introduction: Cerimetry, also known as cerimetric titration, is a type of redox titration that uses cerium(IV) as the titrant. Cerium(IV) is a powerful

oxidizing agent, and cerimetric titration is commonly used to determine the concentration of reducing agents in a sample. This method is widely applied in the analysis of pharmaceuticals, water treatment, and various industrial processes.

Principle: Cerimetry is based on the reduction of cerium(IV) (Ce^{4+}) to cerium(III) (Ce^{3+}) by the reducing agent in the sample. The endpoint of the titration is detected either visually using an appropriate indicator or potentiometrically using an electrode.

Chemical Reactions: $Ce^{4+} + e- \rightarrow Ce^{3+}$

Common Reactions:

- **Oxidation**: The reducing agent in the sample is oxidized.
- **Reduction**: Cerium(IV) is reduced to cerium(III).

Procedure for Cerimetric Titration:

1. **Preparation of Solutions**:

   - **Titrant**: Prepare a standard solution of cerium(IV) sulfate ($Ce(SO_4)_2$). The solution is usually standardized against a primary standard such as sodium oxalate ($Na_2C_2O_4$).
   - **Sample Solution**: Dissolve the sample containing the reducing agent in distilled water.
   - **Indicator**: Use a suitable indicator such as ferroin or N-phenylanthranilic acid, which changes color at the endpoint.

2. **Standardization of Cerium(IV) Solution**:

   - Weigh an accurately known amount of sodium oxalate (primary standard) and dissolve it in distilled water.
   - Add sulfuric acid to acidify the solution.
   - Titrate with the cerium(IV) solution until the endpoint is reached, indicated by the color change of the indicator.
   - Calculate the exact concentration of the cerium(IV) solution.

3. **Titration of Sample**:

- Pipette a measured volume of the sample solution into a titration flask.
- Add sulfuric acid to maintain an acidic environment (usually pH 1-2).
- Add the indicator to the sample solution.
- Titrate with the standardized cerium(IV) solution while continuously stirring until the endpoint is reached, indicated by the color change of the indicator.

4. **Determining the Endpoint**:

- The endpoint is detected visually by the color change of the indicator.
- Alternatively, the endpoint can be determined potentiometrically using a redox electrode to detect the change in potential.

Applications of Cerimetric Titration:

1. **Pharmaceutical Analysis**:

- Determination of reducing agents in pharmaceutical formulations.
- Analysis of active pharmaceutical ingredients (APIs) that are susceptible to oxidation.

2. **Water Treatment**:

- Measurement of reducing agents such as ferrous iron (Fe^{2+}) in water samples.
- Monitoring and controlling the levels of oxidizable substances in water treatment processes.

3. **Industrial Processes**:

- Analysis of reducing agents in various chemical manufacturing processes.
- Quality control in the production of chemicals that involve redox reactions.

4. **Environmental Analysis**:

- Determination of reducing agents in environmental samples, such as soil and water, to assess pollution levels.

9.2 Types of Redox Titrations
9.2.2 Iodimetry

Introduction: Iodimetry is a type of redox titration where iodine (I_2) is used as the titrant. It is particularly useful for the quantitative analysis of reducing agents. Iodimetry involves the direct titration of iodine against a reducing agent, which is then oxidized. The endpoint of the titration is typically detected using starch as an indicator, which forms a blue complex with iodine.

Principle: Iodimetry is based on the oxidation-reduction reaction between iodine and a reducing agent. In this method, iodine is reduced to iodide ions (I^-) while the reducing agent is oxidized. The endpoint is detected by the disappearance of the blue starch-iodine complex, indicating that all the iodine has reacted.

Chemical Reactions: $I_2 + 2e- \rightarrow 2I^-$

Common Reactions:

- **Oxidation**: The reducing agent is oxidized.
- **Reduction**: Iodine is reduced to iodide.

Procedure for Iodimetric Titration:

1. **Preparation of Solutions**:

   - **Titrant**: Prepare a standard solution of iodine. This can be done by dissolving iodine in a potassium iodide (KI) solution to increase its solubility.
   - **Sample Solution**: Dissolve the sample containing the reducing agent in distilled water.
   - **Indicator**: Use starch as an indicator, which forms a blue complex with iodine.

2. **Standardization of Iodine Solution**:

   - Weigh an accurately known amount of a primary standard such as arsenic trioxide (As_2O_3) or sodium thiosulfate ($Na_2S_2O_3$) and dissolve it

in distilled water.
- Titrate with the iodine solution until the endpoint is reached, indicated by the formation of a blue starch-iodine complex.
- Calculate the exact concentration of the iodine solution.

3. **Titration of Sample**:

- Pipette a measured volume of the sample solution into a titration flask.
- Add a few drops of starch indicator to the sample solution.
- Titrate with the standardized iodine solution while continuously stirring until the endpoint is reached, indicated by the appearance of a blue color.

4. **Determining the Endpoint**:

- The endpoint is detected by the formation of the blue starch-iodine complex.
- Continue titration until the blue color persists, indicating the presence of excess iodine and the completion of the reaction with the reducing agent.

Applications of Iodimetric Titration:

1. **Pharmaceutical Analysis**:

- Determination of reducing agents in pharmaceutical formulations.
- Analysis of vitamin C (ascorbic acid) content in dietary supplements.

2. **Food and Beverage Industry**:

- Measurement of antioxidant capacity in food and beverages.
- Analysis of sulfite content in wine and other beverages.

3. **Environmental Analysis**:

- Determination of dissolved oxygen in water samples using the Winkler method.

- Analysis of reducing agents in industrial effluents.

4. **Industrial Processes**:

  - Quality control in the production of chemicals involving redox reactions.
  - Monitoring the concentration of reducing agents in various industrial processes.

9.2 Types of Redox Titrations
9.2.3 Iodometry

Introduction: Iodometry is a type of redox titration in which iodine (I_2) is either produced or consumed during the reaction. This method is often used for the indirect determination of oxidizing agents by titrating with a reducing agent, typically sodium thiosulfate ($Na_2S_2O_3$). Iodometry is widely used in various fields, including pharmaceutical analysis, water treatment, and industrial processes.

Principle: In iodometry, an oxidizing agent reacts with excess iodide ions (I^-) to produce iodine (I_2). The liberated iodine is then titrated with a standard solution of sodium thiosulfate until the endpoint is reached. Starch is used as an indicator, forming a blue complex with iodine, which disappears at the endpoint.

Chemical Reactions:

- **Oxidation Reaction**: Oxidizing agent$+2I^- \rightarrow$Reduced product$+I_2$
- **Reduction Reaction**: $I_2+2S_2O_3^{2-} \rightarrow 2I^-+S_4O_6^{2-}$
- **Procedure for Iodometric Titration**:

1. **Preparation of Solutions**:

  - **Sample Solution**: Dissolve the sample containing the oxidizing agent in distilled water.
  - **Iodine Solution**: Add an excess of potassium iodide (KI) to the sample solution to liberate iodine from the oxidizing agent.
  - **Titrant**: Prepare a standard solution of sodium thiosulfate ($Na_2S_2O_3$).
  - **Indicator**: Use starch as an indicator, which forms a blue complex with iodine.

2. **Standardization of Sodium Thiosulfate Solution**:

- Weigh an accurately known amount of potassium dichromate ($K_2Cr_2O_7$) as a primary standard and dissolve it in distilled water.
- Add an excess of potassium iodide and acidify with sulfuric acid to liberate iodine.
- Titrate the liberated iodine with the sodium thiosulfate solution until the blue color of the starch-iodine complex disappears.
- Calculate the exact concentration of the sodium thiosulfate solution.

3. **Titration of Sample**:

- Pipette a measured volume of the sample solution into a titration flask.
- Add an excess of potassium iodide to the sample solution to liberate iodine from the oxidizing agent.
- Add a few drops of starch indicator to the sample solution.
- Titrate with the standardized sodium thiosulfate solution while continuously stirring until the blue color of the starch-iodine complex disappears.

4. **Determining the Endpoint**:

- The endpoint is detected by the disappearance of the blue starch-iodine complex.
- Continue titration until the solution becomes colorless, indicating the complete reaction of iodine with sodium thiosulfate.

Applications of Iodometric Titration:

1. **Pharmaceutical Analysis**:

- Determination of oxidizing agents in pharmaceutical formulations.
- Analysis of drugs and active pharmaceutical ingredients (APIs) that are susceptible to reduction.

2. **Water Treatment**:

- ○ Measurement of chlorine content in water samples.
- ○ Determination of other oxidizing agents used in disinfection processes.

3. **Industrial Processes**:

- ○ Quality control in the production of chemicals involving redox reactions.
- ○ Monitoring the concentration of oxidizing agents in various industrial processes.

4. **Environmental Analysis**:

- ○ Determination of oxidizing agents in environmental samples, such as soil and water, to assess pollution levels.

9.2 Types of Redox Titrations

9.2.4 Bromatometry

Introduction: Bromatometry is a type of redox titration that involves the use of bromine (Br_2) or bromate (BrO^{3-}) as the titrant. This method is particularly useful for the quantitative analysis of reducing agents and is applied in various fields, including pharmaceuticals, food chemistry, and environmental analysis. Bromine, being a strong oxidizing agent, reacts readily with many reducing agents, making bromatometric titration a reliable method for their determination.

Principle: Bromatometry is based on the oxidation-reduction reaction between bromine (or bromate) and a reducing agent. Bromine is reduced to bromide ions (Br^-) while the reducing agent is oxidized. The endpoint of the titration can be detected using different indicators or by potentiometric methods.

Chemical Reactions:

- **Oxidation Reaction**: $Br_2 + 2e^- \rightarrow 2Br^-$
- **Reduction Reaction**: $BrO^{3-} + 6H^+ + 6e^- \rightarrow Br^- + 3H_2O$
- **Procedure for Bromatometric Titration**:

1. **Preparation of Solutions**:

- **Titrant**: Prepare a standard solution of bromine (Br_2) or potassium bromate ($KBrO_3$). For potassium bromate, dissolve it in water and acidify with sulfuric acid to generate bromine in situ.
- **Sample Solution**: Dissolve the sample containing the reducing agent in distilled water.
- **Indicator**: Use a suitable indicator such as methyl orange, which changes color at the endpoint, or use a potentiometric method for more precise detection.

2. **Standardization of Bromine Solution**:

- Weigh an accurately known amount of a primary standard such as arsenic trioxide (As_2O_3) or sodium thiosulfate ($Na_2S_2O_3$) and dissolve it in distilled water.
- Add an excess of potassium iodide (KI) to liberate iodine by reaction with bromine.
- Titrate the liberated iodine with sodium thiosulfate solution until the endpoint is reached, indicated by the disappearance of the blue starch-iodine complex.
- Calculate the exact concentration of the bromine solution.

3. **Titration of Sample**:

- Pipette a measured volume of the sample solution into a titration flask.
- Add an appropriate indicator to the sample solution.
- Titrate with the standardized bromine solution while continuously stirring until the endpoint is reached, indicated by the color change of the indicator or by a steady potential reading in potentiometric titration.

4. **Determining the Endpoint**:

- The endpoint is detected by the color change of the indicator.
- Alternatively, the endpoint can be determined potentiometrically using a redox electrode to detect the change in potential.

Applications of Bromatometric Titration:

1. **Pharmaceutical Analysis**:

   - Determination of reducing agents in pharmaceutical formulations.
   - Analysis of active pharmaceutical ingredients (APIs) that are susceptible to oxidation.

2. **Food Chemistry**:

   - Measurement of reducing sugars and other antioxidants in food products.
   - Determination of ascorbic acid (vitamin C) content in fruits and vegetables.

3. **Environmental Analysis**:

   - Determination of reducing agents in water and wastewater samples.
   - Analysis of pollutants and contaminants that undergo redox reactions.

4. **Industrial Processes**:

   - Quality control in the production of chemicals involving redox reactions.
   - Monitoring the concentration of reducing agents in various industrial processes.

9.2 Types of Redox Titrations
9.2.5 Dichrometry

Introduction: Dichrometry, also known as dichromate titration, is a type of redox titration that uses potassium dichromate ($K_2Cr_2O_7$) as the titrant. Potassium dichromate is a strong oxidizing agent, and dichromate titration is commonly used for the quantitative analysis of reducing agents. This method is widely applied in environmental analysis, industrial processes, and pharmaceutical analysis.

Principle: Dichrometry is based on the oxidation-reduction reaction between dichromate ions ($Cr_2O_7^{2-}$) and a reducing agent. Potassium dichromate is reduced to chromium(III) ions (Cr^{3+}) while the reducing agent is oxidized. The endpoint of the titration can be detected using an

appropriate indicator or potentiometrically using an electrode.
Chemical Reactions:

- **Oxidation Reaction:** $Cr_2O_7^{2-} + 14H+ + 6e- \rightarrow 2Cr^{3+} + 7H_2O$
- **Reduction Reaction:** Reducing agent $\rightarrow$ Oxidized product + ne-
- **Procedure for Dichrometric Titration:**

1. **Preparation of Solutions:**

   - **Titrant:** Prepare a standard solution of potassium dichromate ($K_2Cr_2O_7$). The solution is usually standardized against a primary standard such as sodium oxalate ($Na_2C_2O_4$).
   - **Sample Solution:** Dissolve the sample containing the reducing agent in distilled water.
   - **Indicator:** Use a suitable indicator such as diphenylamine sulfonate or N-phenylanthranilic acid, which changes color at the endpoint, or use a potentiometric method for more precise detection.

2. **Standardization of Potassium Dichromate Solution:**

   - Weigh an accurately known amount of sodium oxalate (primary standard) and dissolve it in distilled water.
   - Add sulfuric acid to acidify the solution.
   - Titrate with the potassium dichromate solution until the endpoint is reached, indicated by the color change of the indicator.
   - Calculate the exact concentration of the potassium dichromate solution.

3. **Titration of Sample:**

   - Pipette a measured volume of the sample solution into a titration flask.
   - Add sulfuric acid to maintain an acidic environment (usually pH 1-2).
   - Add the indicator to the sample solution.
   - Titrate with the standardized potassium dichromate solution while continuously stirring until the endpoint is reached, indicated by the color change of the indicator or by a steady potential reading in potentiometric titration.

4. **Determining the Endpoint**:

   - The endpoint is detected by the color change of the indicator.
   - Alternatively, the endpoint can be determined potentiometrically using a redox electrode to detect the change in potential.

Applications of Dichrometric Titration:

1. **Environmental Analysis**:

   - Determination of chemical oxygen demand (COD) in water samples to assess pollution levels.
   - Analysis of reducing agents in wastewater and industrial effluents.

2. **Pharmaceutical Analysis**:

   - Determination of reducing agents in pharmaceutical formulations.
   - Analysis of active pharmaceutical ingredients (APIs) that are susceptible to oxidation.

3. **Industrial Processes**:

   - Quality control in the production of chemicals involving redox reactions.
   - Monitoring the concentration of reducing agents in various industrial processes.

4. **Food and Beverage Industry**:

   - Measurement of reducing sugars and other antioxidants in food products.
   - Determination of ascorbic acid (vitamin C) content in fruits and vegetables.

9.2 Types of Redox Titrations

9.2.6 Titration with Potassium Iodate

Introduction: Titration with potassium iodate (KIO_3) is a form of redox titration where potassium iodate acts as the titrant. Potassium iodate is a strong oxidizing agent and is often used for the determination of reducing agents. This method is particularly useful in various fields such as pharmaceutical analysis, environmental testing, and food chemistry.

Principle: The principle of iodate titration involves the reaction between potassium iodate and a reducing agent. During the titration, potassium iodate oxidizes the reducing agent and itself gets reduced to iodide ions (I^-). The liberated iodine (I_2) can then be titrated with sodium thiosulfate ($Na_2S_2O_3$) using starch as an indicator to detect the endpoint.

Chemical Reactions:

- **Oxidation Reaction**: $IO_3^- + 6H^+ + 6e^- \rightarrow I^- + 3H_2O$
- **Reduction Reaction**:
- Reducing agent $\rightarrow$ Oxidized product $+ ne^-$
- **Iodine Formation**: $IO_3^- + 5I^- + 6H^+ \rightarrow 3I_2 + 3H_2O$
- **Procedure for Titration with Potassium Iodate**:

1. **Preparation of Solutions**:

    - **Titrant**: Prepare a standard solution of potassium iodate (KIO_3).
    - **Sample Solution**: Dissolve the sample containing the reducing agent in distilled water.
    - **Indicator**: Use starch as an indicator, which forms a blue complex with iodine.

2. **Standardization of Potassium Iodate Solution**:

    - Weigh an accurately known amount of a primary standard such as sodium thiosulfate ($Na_2S_2O_3$) and dissolve it in distilled water.
    - Add an excess of potassium iodide (KI) and sulfuric acid (H_2SO_4) to the solution.
    - The potassium iodate reacts with potassium iodide in the presence of acid to produce iodine.
    - Titrate the liberated iodine with the sodium thiosulfate solution until the blue color of the starch-iodine complex disappears.
    - Calculate the exact concentration of the potassium iodate solution.

3. **Titration of Sample**:

- Pipette a measured volume of the sample solution into a titration flask.
- Add an excess of potassium iodide and acidify the solution with sulfuric acid to liberate iodine from the reaction with potassium iodate.
- Add a few drops of starch indicator to the sample solution.
- Titrate the liberated iodine with the standardized sodium thiosulfate solution while continuously stirring until the blue color of the starch-iodine complex disappears.

4. **Determining the Endpoint**:

- The endpoint is detected by the disappearance of the blue starch-iodine complex.
- Continue titration until the solution becomes colorless, indicating the complete reaction of iodine with sodium thiosulfate.

Applications of Titration with Potassium Iodate:

1. **Pharmaceutical Analysis**:

- Determination of reducing agents in pharmaceutical formulations.
- Analysis of active pharmaceutical ingredients (APIs) that are susceptible to oxidation.

2. **Environmental Analysis**:

- Determination of oxidizable substances in water samples.
- Analysis of pollutants and contaminants that undergo redox reactions.

3. **Food Chemistry**:

- Measurement of reducing sugars and other antioxidants in food products.
- Determination of ascorbic acid (vitamin C) content in fruits and vegetables.

4. **Industrial Processes**:

- Quality control in the production of chemicals involving redox reactions.
- Monitoring the concentration of reducing agents in various industrial processes.

TEN
ELECTROCHEMICAL METHODS OF ANALYSIS

10.1 Conductometry

10.1.1 Introduction and Principles

Introduction: Conductometry is an analytical technique used to measure the electrical conductivity of a solution. This method is based on the principle that the conductivity of a solution changes as ions move under the influence of an electric field. Conductometry is widely used in various fields, including environmental monitoring, pharmaceutical analysis, and industrial processes, due to its simplicity, sensitivity, and accuracy.

Principle: The principle of conductometry revolves around the measurement of electrical conductivity, which is the ability of a solution to conduct an electric current. Conductivity is directly proportional to the concentration of ions in the solution. The more ions present, the higher the conductivity. This technique involves applying an alternating current (AC) through a solution and measuring the resulting current flow.

Key Concepts:

1. **Conductance (G)**: Conductance is the ability of a solution to conduct an electric current and is measured in siemens (S). It is the reciprocal of resistance (R): G=1/ R **Conductivity (κ)**: Conductivity is a measure of the conductance of a solution normalized to the unit length and cross-sectional area of the solution. It is measured in siemens per meter (S/m). The relationship between conductance and conductivity is given by: κ=G·l/A where:

- ∘ κ is the conductivity,
- ∘ G is the conductance,
- ∘ l is the distance between the electrodes,
- ∘ A is the cross-sectional area of the solution between the electrodes.

2. **Molar Conductivity (Λm)**: Molar conductivity is the conductivity of a solution containing one mole of electrolyte per liter. It is calculated using the formula: $\Lambda m = \kappa / C$ where:

- ∘ Λm is the molar conductivity,
- ∘ κ is the conductivity,
- ∘ C is the concentration of the electrolyte in moles per liter.

Conductometric Measurements:

1. **Apparatus**: The primary apparatus for conductometric measurements includes a conductometric cell (containing electrodes), a conductivity meter, and a source of alternating current (AC).
2. **Procedure**:

- ∘ Prepare the sample solution and pour it into the conductometric cell.
- ∘ Calibrate the conductivity meter using standard solutions with known conductivity values.
- ∘ Immerse the electrodes into the sample solution.
- ∘ Apply an AC voltage to the electrodes and measure the resulting current flow.
- ∘ The conductivity meter calculates the conductance based on the current flow and displays the conductivity of the solution.

3. **Types of Conductometric Titrations**:

- ∘ **Strong Acid-Strong Base Titrations**: Involve titrating a strong acid with a strong base or vice versa. The conductivity changes significantly at the equivalence point due to the complete neutralization of ions.
- ∘ **Weak Acid-Strong Base Titrations**: Involve titrating a weak acid with a strong base. The conductivity changes gradually and is less pronounced at the equivalence point.

- **Precipitation Titrations**: Involve the formation of a precipitate during the titration. The conductivity decreases as the ions are removed from the solution to form an insoluble compound.

Applications of Conductometry:

1. **Environmental Monitoring**:

   - Measurement of water purity by determining the conductivity of natural waters, wastewater, and drinking water.
   - Detection of pollutants and monitoring of water quality.

2. **Pharmaceutical Analysis**:

   - Determination of the purity and concentration of pharmaceutical compounds.
   - Analysis of electrolytes in pharmaceutical formulations.

3. **Industrial Processes**:

   - Monitoring the concentration of ions in industrial solutions, such as plating baths and cooling waters.
   - Quality control in the production of chemicals and food products.

4. **Academic Research**:

   - Study of ionization and dissociation constants of acids, bases, and salts.
   - Investigation of the properties of electrolytes in solution.

Advantages of Conductometry:

- **Simplicity**: Conductometric measurements are straightforward and do not require complex sample preparation.
- **Sensitivity**: Conductometry can detect low concentrations of ions in a solution.
- **Non-destructive**: The technique does not alter the sample, allowing for further analysis if needed.

- **Versatility**: Applicable to a wide range of solutions and titrations.

10.1 Conductometry
10.1.2 Conductometric Titrations

Introduction: Conductometric titrations are a subset of conductometry where the change in the electrical conductivity of a solution is monitored during the course of a titration. This technique is particularly useful when dealing with colored or turbid solutions where traditional visual indicators might be ineffective. Conductometric titrations are versatile and can be applied to a wide range of chemical reactions, including acid-base, precipitation, and complexometric titrations.

Principle: The principle of conductometric titrations is based on the change in the number of ions in the solution during a titration process. As the titrant is added to the analyte solution, the conductivity changes depending on the nature and concentration of the ions present. By plotting the conductivity against the volume of titrant added, the endpoint of the titration can be determined from the point of inflection on the graph.

Types of Conductometric Titrations:

1. **Strong Acid-Strong Base Titrations**:

   - **Reaction**: $HCl + NaOH \rightarrow NaCl + H_2O$
   - **Principle**: Initially, the conductivity decreases as H^+ ions are neutralized by OH- ions to form water, which has low conductivity. After the equivalence point, the addition of excess OH- ions increases the conductivity.
   - **Plot**: The conductivity vs. volume of NaOH added shows a V-shaped curve with the lowest point indicating the equivalence point.

2. **Weak Acid-Strong Base Titrations**:

   - **Reaction**: $CH_3COOH + NaOH \rightarrow CH_3COONa + H_2O$
   - **Principle**: The conductivity changes more gradually compared to strong acid-strong base titrations because the weak acid partially ionizes. The equivalence point is determined by the intersection of the two linear portions of the conductivity vs. volume curve.
   - **Plot**: The plot shows a gradual increase in conductivity before the equivalence point due to the formation of the weak acid's salt,

followed by a steeper increase after the equivalence point.

3. **Precipitation Titrations**:

   - **Reaction**: $AgNO_3 + NaCl \rightarrow AgCl\downarrow + NaNO_3$
   - **Principle**: The conductivity decreases as the ions precipitate out of the solution. After the equivalence point, the addition of excess titrant increases the conductivity again.
   - **Plot**: The plot shows a decrease in conductivity as the precipitate forms, followed by an increase after the equivalence point when excess titrant is added.

4. **Complexometric Titrations**:

   - **Reaction**: $Ca^{2+} + EDTA^{4-} \rightarrow Ca\text{-}EDTA$
   - **Principle**: The conductivity changes as the metal ions form complexes with the titrant (EDTA). The endpoint is determined from the change in slope of the conductivity vs. volume plot.
   - **Plot**: The plot shows a change in conductivity corresponding to the formation of the metal-ligand complex, with the endpoint indicated by a change in the slope.

Procedure for Conductometric Titrations:

1. **Preparation**:

   - Prepare the analyte solution and place it in a conductometric cell.
   - Calibrate the conductivity meter with standard solutions.

2. **Titration**:

   - Add the titrant gradually to the analyte solution while continuously stirring.
   - Record the conductivity of the solution after each addition of the titrant.

3. **Plotting and Analysis**:

- Plot the conductivity against the volume of titrant added.
- Determine the endpoint from the plot by identifying the point of inflection or the intersection of linear segments.

Example Calculation:
Titration of HCl with NaOH:

1. **Initial Data:**

   - Volume of HCl solution: 50 mL
   - Initial conductivity of HCl solution: κi\kappa_iκi
   - Molarity of NaOH solution: 0.1 M

2. **Procedure:**

   - Add NaOH solution incrementally to the HCl solution.
   - Measure and record the conductivity after each addition.
   - Plot conductivity vs. volume of NaOH added.

3. **Determination of Endpoint:**

   - From the plot, identify the volume of NaOH at the minimum conductivity.
   - Use this volume to calculate the concentration of HCl.

Applications of Conductometric Titrations:

1. **Environmental Analysis:**

   - Determination of pollutants in water by precipitation titrations.
   - Analysis of acid rain by titrating acidic components.

2. **Pharmaceutical Analysis:**

   - Determination of the purity and concentration of active pharmaceutical ingredients.
   - Analysis of complex formulations where traditional indicators might interfere.

3. **Industrial Processes**:

   ○ Quality control in the production of chemicals and food products.
   ○ Monitoring ion concentrations in various industrial solutions.

4. **Research and Development**:

   ○ Investigation of ionization and dissociation constants of acids, bases, and salts.
   ○ Study of complex formation reactions and their kinetics.

Advantages of Conductometric Titrations:

- **Non-reliance on Visual Indicators**: Useful for colored or turbid solutions.
- **Precision**: Accurate determination of endpoints, especially in weak acid-strong base titrations.
- **Versatility**: Applicable to a wide range of reactions including acid-base, precipitation, and complexometric titrations.

10.1 Conductometry

10.1.3 Applications

Introduction: Conductometry, due to its simplicity and sensitivity, finds extensive applications across various fields. It is particularly useful in situations where traditional visual indicators are ineffective, and precise measurements of ionic concentrations are required. Below are some of the primary applications of conductometry.

Applications of Conductometry:

1. **Environmental Monitoring**:

   ○ **Water Quality Assessment**: Conductometry is widely used to measure the purity of water by determining its conductivity. High conductivity indicates a high concentration of dissolved ions, which can signify pollution or the presence of impurities.
   ○ **Detection of Pollutants**: Conductometric titrations can be used to detect and quantify pollutants such as heavy metals, nitrates, and phosphates in water bodies. For example, the determination of

chloride concentration in wastewater by titration with silver nitrate.

2. **Pharmaceutical Analysis**:

   - **Determination of Drug Purity**: Conductometric titrations are employed to determine the purity and concentration of active pharmaceutical ingredients (APIs) in drugs. This is particularly useful for drugs that do not have a clear visual endpoint.
   - **Analysis of Electrolytes**: Conductometry is used to analyze the concentration of electrolytes in pharmaceutical formulations, ensuring they meet the required specifications.

3. **Industrial Processes**:

   - **Quality Control**: In industries such as food, beverage, and chemical manufacturing, conductometry is used to monitor the concentration of ions in various solutions. For instance, it helps in controlling the quality of products by ensuring that the concentration of ingredients is within specified limits.
   - **Monitoring of Plating Baths**: In electroplating industries, conductometry is used to monitor and control the concentration of metal ions in plating baths, ensuring optimal plating conditions and product quality.

4. **Food and Beverage Industry**:

   - **Determination of Salt Content**: Conductometric titrations are used to determine the salt content in food products. This is crucial for both quality control and regulatory compliance.
   - **Measurement of Acidity**: The acidity of juices, wines, and other beverages can be determined by titration with a strong base, and the endpoint can be detected conductometrically.

5. **Academic Research**:

   - **Study of Ionization Constants**: Conductometry is used in research to study the ionization and dissociation constants of acids, bases, and salts. This information is vital for understanding chemical equilibria in solutions.

- **Investigation of Reaction Kinetics**: Conductometric methods are employed to investigate the kinetics of chemical reactions, particularly those involving ionic species.

6. **Medical Applications**:

- **Analysis of Body Fluids**: Conductometry is used to analyze the electrolyte content in body fluids such as blood and urine. This is important for diagnosing and monitoring various medical conditions, including electrolyte imbalances.

7. **Agriculture**:

- **Soil Analysis**: The conductivity of soil extracts is measured to determine the concentration of soluble salts, which affects soil fertility and crop yield. This helps in making informed decisions about fertilizer application.

8. **Environmental Science**:

- **Acid Rain Analysis**: Conductometric titration is used to determine the concentration of acidic components in rainwater, which is essential for studying the effects of acid rain on the environment.

Advantages of Conductometric Applications:

- **Non-destructive Analysis**: Conductometric methods do not alter the sample, allowing for further analysis if needed.
- **High Sensitivity**: Capable of detecting low concentrations of ions, making it suitable for trace analysis.
- **Wide Range of Applications**: Applicable to various fields including environmental monitoring, pharmaceutical analysis, industrial processes, and academic research.
- **No Need for Indicators**: Eliminates the need for visual indicators, which is beneficial for colored or turbid solutions.

10.2 Potentiometry

10.2.1 Electrochemical Cells

Introduction: Potentiometry is an analytical method that involves the measurement of the potential difference between two electrodes in an electrochemical cell. This technique is used to determine the concentration of ions in a solution by measuring the voltage of the cell. Potentiometry is widely used in various fields, including environmental monitoring, pharmaceuticals, and industrial processes, due to its precision and simplicity.

Principle: The principle of potentiometry is based on the Nernst equation, which relates the potential of an electrochemical cell to the concentration of the ions involved in the redox reaction. The cell potential is measured using a voltmeter, and this potential is used to determine the ion concentration in the sample solution.

Electrochemical Cells: An electrochemical cell consists of two half-cells connected by a salt bridge or a porous membrane. Each half-cell contains an electrode and an electrolyte. There are two main types of electrochemical cells used in potentiometry: galvanic cells and electrolytic cells.

1. **Galvanic Cells**:

   - **Definition**: A galvanic cell, also known as a voltaic cell, is an electrochemical cell that generates electrical energy from a spontaneous redox reaction.
   - **Components**:

     - **Anode**: The electrode where oxidation occurs. Electrons are released into the external circuit.
     - **Cathode**: The electrode where reduction occurs. Electrons are accepted from the external circuit.
     - **Salt Bridge**: A device that maintains electrical neutrality by allowing the flow of ions between the two half-cells.

   - **Example**: Daniell Cell

     - Anode reaction: $Zn \rightarrow Zn^{2+} + 2e-$
     - Cathode reaction: $Cu^{2+} + 2e- \rightarrow Cu$
     - Overall reaction: $Zn + Cu^{2+} \rightarrow Zn^{2+} + Cu$

2. **Electrolytic Cells**:

- **Definition**: An electrolytic cell is an electrochemical cell that uses electrical energy to drive a non-spontaneous redox reaction.
- **Components**:

  - **Anode**: The electrode where oxidation occurs. Electrons are pulled from the anode by the external power source.
  - **Cathode**: The electrode where reduction occurs. Electrons are supplied to the cathode by the external power source.
  - **Power Source**: Provides the electrical energy needed to drive the non-spontaneous reaction.

- **Example**: Electrolysis of Water

  - Anode reaction: $2H_2O \rightarrow O_2 + 4H^+ + 4\,e-$
  - Cathode reaction: $4H^+ + 4e- \rightarrow 2H_2$
  - Overall reaction: $2H_2O \rightarrow 2H_2 + O_2$
  - **Construction and Working of Reference and Indicator Electrodes**:

3. **Reference Electrodes**:

- **Standard Hydrogen Electrode (SHE)**:

  - Construction: Consists of a platinum electrode in contact with 1 M H^+ ions and bathed in hydrogen gas at 1 atm pressure.
  - Working: The potential of the SHE is defined as 0.00 V, and it serves as a standard for measuring the potential of other electrodes.

- **Silver/Silver Chloride Electrode (Ag/AgCl)**:

  - Construction: Consists of a silver wire coated with silver chloride, immersed in a solution of potassium chloride.
  - Working: The electrode potential is stable and reproducible, making it suitable for use as a reference electrode.

- ○ **Calomel Electrode**:

  - Construction: Consists of mercury in contact with mercurous chloride (calomel), immersed in a solution of potassium chloride.
  - Working: The potential of the calomel electrode is well-defined and commonly used in potentiometric measurements.

4. **Indicator Electrodes**:

   - ○ **Metal Electrodes**:

     - Construction: Made of inert metals such as platinum or gold, which do not participate in the redox reaction.
     - Working: The potential of the metal electrode changes in response to the concentration of the redox species in the solution.

   - ○ **Ion-Selective Electrodes (ISEs)**:

     - Construction: Consist of a membrane that is selective to a specific ion. The membrane can be glass (e.g., pH electrode), polymer, or crystalline.
     - Working: The potential difference across the membrane is proportional to the concentration of the target ion in the solution.
     - Example: pH electrode, fluoride ion-selective electrode.

Nernst Equation: The Nernst equation relates the electrode potential to the concentration of the ions involved in the redox reaction: $E = E° + (RT / nF) * \ln([Red] / [Ox])$
Where:

- E is the cell potential (voltage).
- E° is the standard electrode potential.
- R is the universal gas constant (8.314 J/(molK)).
- T is the temperature in Kelvin.
- n is the number of moles of electrons transferred in the reaction.
- F is the Faraday constant (96485 C/mol).
- ln is the natural logarithm.
- [Red] is the concentration of the reduced form of the species.

- [Ox] is the concentration of the oxidized form of the species.

Applications of Electrochemical Cells in Potentiometry:

1. **Environmental Monitoring**:

   - Measurement of pH in natural waters to assess acidity and alkalinity.
   - Determination of ion concentrations in water samples, such as nitrate, chloride, and fluoride.

2. **Pharmaceutical Analysis**:

   - Determination of the concentration of active pharmaceutical ingredients (APIs) in drug formulations.
   - Monitoring of pH and ionic strength in pharmaceutical products to ensure stability and efficacy.

3. **Industrial Processes**:

   - Monitoring and control of pH in chemical manufacturing processes.
   - Determination of ion concentrations in industrial effluents and wastewater treatment.

4. **Food and Beverage Industry**:

   - Measurement of pH in food and beverages to ensure product quality and safety.
   - Determination of ion concentrations, such as sodium and potassium, in food products.

5. **Research and Development**:

   - Study of redox reactions and electrochemical properties of various compounds.
   - Investigation of ion-selective membranes and development of new ion-selective electrodes.

10.2 Potentiometry

10.2.2 Construction and Working of Reference Electrodes

Introduction: Reference electrodes are essential components in potentiometric measurements, providing a stable and known potential against which the potential of the indicator electrode can be measured. The accuracy and reliability of potentiometric measurements depend on the stability and reproducibility of the reference electrode. Commonly used reference electrodes include the Standard Hydrogen Electrode (SHE), Silver/ Silver Chloride (Ag/AgCl) Electrode, and Calomel Electrode.

Standard Hydrogen Electrode (SHE):

1. **Construction:**

   - The SHE consists of a platinum electrode coated with a thin layer of platinum black to increase the surface area.
   - The platinum electrode is immersed in an acidic solution (typically 1 M HCl) containing 1 M hydrogen ions (H^+).
   - Hydrogen gas (H_2) is bubbled over the platinum electrode at a pressure of 1 atmosphere.
   - The setup ensures a constant activity of hydrogen ions and hydrogen gas in contact with the platinum surface.

2. **Working:**

   - The SHE is based on the half-reaction: $H_2 \rightarrow 2H^+ + 2\,e-$
   - The potential of the SHE is defined as 0.00 V at all temperatures.
   - The SHE serves as a universal reference point for measuring the potentials of other electrodes.
   - Due to its defined potential, the SHE is used to calibrate other reference electrodes and to determine standard electrode potentials.

Silver/Silver Chloride Electrode (Ag/AgCl):

1. **Construction:**

   - The Ag/AgCl electrode consists of a silver wire coated with a layer of silver chloride.
   - The coated wire is immersed in a solution of potassium chloride (KCl) of known concentration.

- A porous frit or junction allows ionic contact between the reference electrode and the sample solution.

2. **Working:**

- The half-reaction for the Ag/AgCl electrode is: $AgCl + e^- \rightarrow Ag + Cl^-$
- The potential of the Ag/AgCl electrode depends on the concentration of the KCl solution. Commonly used concentrations are 0.1 M, 1 M, and saturated KCl.
- The potential of the Ag/AgCl electrode relative to the SHE can be calculated using the Nernst equation: $E(Ag/AgCl) = E°(Ag/AgCl) - (RT / F) * \ln([Cl^-])$
- The Ag/AgCl electrode provides a stable and reproducible potential, making it widely used in potentiometric measurements.

Calomel Electrode:

1. **Construction:**

- The calomel electrode consists of mercury (Hg) in contact with mercurous chloride (Hg_2Cl_2), also known as calomel.
- The Hg/ Hg_2Cl_2 mixture is in contact with a solution of potassium chloride (KCl) of known concentration.
- A porous frit or junction provides ionic contact between the reference electrode and the sample solution.

2. **Working:**

- The half-reaction for the calomel electrode is: $Hg_2Cl_2 + 2 e^- \rightarrow 2Hg + 2Cl^-$ The potential of the calomel electrode depends on the concentration of the KCl solution. Commonly used concentrations are saturated KCl, 1 M KCl, and 0.1 M KCl.
- The potential of the calomel electrode relative to the SHE can be calculated using the Nernst equation: $E(Ag/AgCl) = E°(Ag/AgCl) - (RT / F) * \ln([Cl^-])$
- The calomel electrode provides a stable and well-defined potential, making it suitable for various potentiometric applications.

Applications of Reference Electrodes:

1. **Environmental Monitoring**:

   - Measurement of pH and ion concentrations in natural waters, wastewater, and soil samples.
   - Determination of pollutants and contaminants in environmental samples.

2. **Pharmaceutical Analysis**:

   - Quality control of pharmaceutical products by measuring the pH and ion concentrations.
   - Monitoring the stability and potency of drug formulations.

3. **Industrial Processes**:

   - Control and monitoring of pH and ion concentrations in chemical manufacturing processes.
   - Quality assurance in the production of food and beverages.

4. **Research and Development**:

   - Study of redox reactions and electrochemical properties of compounds.
   - Investigation of ion-selective membranes and development of new electrodes.

Advantages of Reference Electrodes:

- **Stability**: Provide a stable and reproducible potential, essential for accurate potentiometric measurements.
- **Versatility**: Suitable for a wide range of applications, from environmental monitoring to pharmaceutical analysis.
- **Ease of Use**: Simple to construct and maintain, making them convenient for routine laboratory use.

10.2 Potentiometry

10.2.4 Potentiometric Titrations

Introduction: Potentiometric titrations are a type of titration where the potential (voltage) of the solution is measured using a potentiometer or a pH meter to determine the endpoint. This technique is particularly useful for titrations where traditional indicators are not effective, such as in colored or turbid solutions. Potentiometric titrations can be applied to various types of reactions, including acid-base, redox, precipitation, and complexometric titrations.

Principle: The principle of potentiometric titrations is based on the measurement of the potential difference between two electrodes immersed in the solution. The potential changes as the titrant is added and reaches a significant change at the equivalence point. This change in potential is used to accurately determine the endpoint of the titration.

Types of Potentiometric Titrations:

1. **Acid-Base Titrations**:

    - **Strong Acid-Strong Base**: The titration of a strong acid with a strong base or vice versa. The pH changes sharply at the equivalence point.

        - **Example**: Titration of hydrochloric acid (HCl) with sodium hydroxide (NaOH).

    - **Weak Acid-Strong Base**: The titration of a weak acid with a strong base. The pH change is more gradual, and the equivalence point occurs at a pH greater than 7.

        - **Example**: Titration of acetic acid (CH_3COOH) with sodium hydroxide (NaOH).

2. **Redox Titrations**:

    - **Oxidation-Reduction Reactions**: The titration involves redox reactions where the potential of the solution changes significantly at the equivalence point.

        - **Example**: Titration of ferrous ions (Fe^{2+}) with potassium permanganate ($KMnO_4$).

3. **Precipitation Titrations**:

   - **Formation of Precipitates**: The titration involves the formation of an insoluble precipitate. The potential changes as the ions are removed from the solution.

     - **Example**: Titration of chloride ions (Cl^-) with silver nitrate ($AgNO_3$).

4. **Complexometric Titrations**:

   - **Complex Formation**: The titration involves the formation of a complex between the titrant and the analyte. The potential changes as the complex forms.

     - **Example**: Titration of calcium ions (Ca^{2+}) with ethylenediaminetetraacetic acid (EDTA).

   Procedure for Potentiometric Titrations:

1. **Preparation**:

   - Prepare the analyte solution and place it in a titration flask.
   - Calibrate the potentiometer or pH meter using standard buffer solutions if performing an acid-base titration.

2. **Titration**:

   - Immerse the reference and indicator electrodes into the analyte solution.
   - Begin adding the titrant from a burette while continuously stirring the solution.
   - Record the potential (voltage) after each addition of the titrant.

3. **Plotting and Analysis**:

   - Plot the potential (E) or pH against the volume of titrant added.
   - Identify the point of inflection or the sharp change in the plot, which corresponds to the equivalence point.

Example of Potentiometric Titration:
Titration of Hydrochloric Acid with Sodium Hydroxide:

1. **Initial Data**:

   - Volume of HCl solution: 50 mL
   - Molarity of NaOH solution: 0.1 M

2. **Procedure**:

   - Fill the burette with the 0.1 M NaOH solution.
   - Immerse the pH electrode and reference electrode in the HCl solution.
   - Add NaOH solution incrementally to the HCl solution, recording the pH after each addition.

3. **Plotting and Analysis**:

   - Plot pH vs. volume of NaOH added.
   - The equivalence point is determined from the sharp rise in pH at the point where all the HCl has been neutralized.

Applications of Potentiometric Titrations:

1. **Environmental Monitoring**:

   - Determination of pH and ion concentrations in water samples.
   - Measurement of pollutants and contaminants in environmental samples.

2. **Pharmaceutical Analysis**:

   - Determination of drug purity and concentration.
   - Analysis of complex formulations where visual indicators are ineffective.

3. **Industrial Processes**:

- ○ Monitoring and control of pH and ion concentrations in chemical manufacturing.
- ○ Quality assurance in the production of food and beverages.

4. **Academic Research**:

- ○ Study of redox reactions and electrochemical properties of compounds.
- ○ Investigation of acid-base equilibria and complex formation.

Advantages of Potentiometric Titrations:

- **Accuracy**: Provides precise determination of the equivalence point.
- **Versatility**: Applicable to various types of titrations, including acid-base, redox, precipitation, and complexometric titrations.
- **Non-reliance on Visual Indicators**: Suitable for colored or turbid solutions where visual indicators may not be effective.
- **Automation**: Can be easily automated for high-throughput analysis.

10.2 Potentiometry

10.2.5 Applications

Introduction: Potentiometry is a versatile analytical technique that finds applications in a wide range of fields, including environmental monitoring, pharmaceutical analysis, industrial processes, food and beverage industry, and academic research. The technique is valued for its precision, reliability, and ability to measure the concentration of ions without the need for visual indicators.

Applications of Potentiometry:

1. **Environmental Monitoring**:

- ○ **pH Measurement**: Potentiometry is widely used for measuring the pH of natural waters, wastewater, and soil samples. Monitoring pH is crucial for assessing water quality, environmental pollution, and soil health.
- ○ **Ion Concentration Analysis**: Potentiometric methods are employed to determine the concentration of various ions, such as nitrates, chlorides, fluorides, and heavy metals, in environmental samples.

This is essential for pollution control and regulatory compliance.

- **Detection of Contaminants**: Potentiometric sensors can detect and quantify contaminants in water bodies, aiding in the identification of sources of pollution and in the implementation of remediation measures.

2. Pharmaceutical Analysis:

- **Drug Purity and Concentration**: Potentiometric titrations are used to determine the purity and concentration of active pharmaceutical ingredients (APIs) in drug formulations. This ensures that pharmaceutical products meet quality standards and regulatory requirements.
- **pH Monitoring**: The pH of pharmaceutical solutions, creams, and gels is measured potentiometrically to ensure product stability and efficacy. Maintaining the correct pH is crucial for the bioavailability and shelf life of drugs.
- **Analysis of Electrolytes**: Potentiometry is used to analyze the concentration of electrolytes in pharmaceutical products, which is important for the formulation and quality control of electrolyte solutions.

3. Industrial Processes:

- **Quality Control in Chemical Manufacturing**: Potentiometric titrations are used to monitor and control the concentration of reactants and products in chemical manufacturing processes. This ensures that the final products meet the desired specifications.
- **Process Monitoring**: Continuous potentiometric monitoring of pH and ion concentrations is essential in various industrial processes, such as electroplating, fermentation, and water treatment.
- **Corrosion Studies**: Potentiometric methods are used to study the corrosion behavior of metals in different environments. This information is vital for developing corrosion-resistant materials and protective coatings.

4. Food and Beverage Industry:

- ○ **pH Measurement**: Potentiometry is employed to measure the pH of food products and beverages, ensuring product quality, safety, and consistency. pH measurement is particularly important in dairy products, beverages, and processed foods.
- ○ **Determination of Salt Content**: Potentiometric titrations are used to determine the salt content in food products. Accurate salt measurement is crucial for flavor, preservation, and regulatory compliance.
- ○ **Analysis of Additives**: Potentiometry is used to analyze the concentration of food additives, such as preservatives and antioxidants, ensuring they are within the acceptable limits.

5. **Academic Research**:

- ○ **Study of Redox Reactions**: Potentiometric titrations are used in research to study redox reactions and determine the standard electrode potentials of various compounds. This information is essential for understanding the electrochemical behavior of substances.
- ○ **Investigation of Acid-Base Equilibria**: Potentiometric methods are used to investigate the ionization constants of acids and bases, providing insights into their chemical properties and behavior in solution.
- ○ **Development of Ion-Selective Electrodes**: Research in potentiometry includes the development and optimization of ion-selective electrodes (ISEs) for detecting specific ions. These electrodes have applications in various fields, including medical diagnostics and environmental monitoring.

Advantages of Potentiometry:

- **Precision and Accuracy**: Potentiometry provides precise and accurate measurements of ion concentrations and pH levels, making it a reliable analytical technique.
- **Non-Destructive**: The method does not alter the sample, allowing for further analysis if needed.
- **Versatility**: Potentiometry can be applied to a wide range of chemical reactions and sample types, including aqueous and non-aqueous

solutions.

- **No Need for Visual Indicators**: Potentiometric titrations do not rely on visual indicators, making them suitable for colored or turbid solutions where traditional indicators might be ineffective.
- **Automation**: Potentiometric measurements can be easily automated, enabling high-throughput analysis and continuous monitoring.

10.3 Polarography

10.3.1 Principles and Ilkovic Equation

Introduction: Polarography is an electroanalytical technique that involves measuring the current that flows in an electrochemical cell under conditions where the potential of the working electrode is varied. This technique is particularly useful for the analysis of trace metals and organic compounds. The key to polarography is the dropping mercury electrode (DME), which serves as the working electrode.

Principles of Polarography:

1. **Electrochemical Cell Setup**:

   - The polarographic cell consists of a working electrode (usually a dropping mercury electrode), a reference electrode (often a saturated calomel electrode or Ag/AgCl electrode), and an auxiliary electrode (platinum wire).
   - The working electrode's potential is controlled and varied linearly or stepwise, while the current response is measured.

2. **Dropping Mercury Electrode (DME)**:

   - The DME provides a fresh and renewable surface for each measurement, reducing issues related to electrode fouling.
   - Mercury drops from the capillary at a constant rate, forming small, reproducible surfaces for the redox reactions.

3. **Polarogram**:

   - A polarogram is a plot of the current (i) versus the applied potential (E).

- ◦ As the potential is scanned, the current increases due to the reduction or oxidation of analyte species at the DME surface.

4. **Diffusion Current (id):**

- ◦ The diffusion current is the limiting current observed in polarography, resulting from the mass transport of analyte species to the electrode surface.
- ◦ It is proportional to the concentration of the analyte.

Ilkovic Equation: The Ilkovic equation describes the relationship between the diffusion current (id) and the concentration of the analyte. It is given by:

$$id = 607n\, D^{1/2}\, m^{2/3}\, t^{1/6}\, C \quad \text{where:}$$

- $\cdot$ id = diffusion current (μA)
- $\cdot$ n = number of electrons involved in the redox process
- $\cdot$ D = diffusion coefficient of the analyte (cm^2/s)
- $\cdot$ m = rate of mercury drop formation (mg/s)
- $\cdot$ t = drop time (s)
- $\cdot$ C = concentration of the analyte (mol/L)

Explanation of the Ilkovic Equation:

1. **n (Number of Electrons):** The number of electrons transferred in the redox reaction directly affects the magnitude of the current. More electrons result in a higher current.
2. **D (Diffusion Coefficient):** This parameter describes how quickly the analyte molecules diffuse through the solution to the electrode surface. A higher diffusion coefficient leads to a higher current.
3. **m (Rate of Mercury Drop Formation):** The rate at which mercury drops are formed affects the surface area of the electrode, influencing the current. Faster drop formation increases the current.
4. **t (Drop Time):** The time each mercury drop exists before detaching affects the interaction time between the analyte and the electrode. Longer drop times allow more analyte to react, increasing the current.
5. **C (Concentration):** The concentration of the analyte is directly proportional to the diffusion current. Higher concentrations lead to

higher currents.

Applications of Polarography:

1. **Trace Metal Analysis:**

   - Polarography is used to detect and quantify trace levels of metals such as lead, cadmium, zinc, and copper in various samples, including environmental, biological, and industrial samples.

2. **Organic Compound Analysis:**

   - Polarography is applied to analyze organic compounds that can be reduced or oxidized at the electrode, such as vitamins, antibiotics, and pesticides.

3. **Environmental Monitoring:**

   - Monitoring heavy metal pollution in water bodies and soil is a significant application of polarography, helping to ensure environmental safety and compliance with regulations.

4. **Pharmaceutical Analysis:**

   - Determining the concentration of active ingredients and impurities in pharmaceutical formulations can be achieved using polarographic techniques.

5. **Research and Development:**

   - Polarography is used in electrochemical research to study reaction mechanisms, kinetics, and the behavior of electroactive species.

Advantages of Polarography:

- **Sensitivity:** Capable of detecting trace levels of analytes.
- **Selectivity:** Can distinguish between different species based on their redox potentials.

- **Versatility**: Applicable to a wide range of inorganic and organic compounds.
- **Reproducibility**: Provides consistent results due to the renewable surface of the DME.

10.3 Polarography

10.3.2 Dropping Mercury Electrode

Introduction: The Dropping Mercury Electrode (DME) is a key component in polarography, providing a unique and renewable surface for electrochemical reactions. The DME has specific characteristics that make it ideal for certain types of analytical measurements, particularly in trace metal analysis and the study of electrochemical reactions.

Construction and Working:

1. **Construction**:

   - The DME consists of a reservoir of mercury connected to a capillary tube.
   - The mercury flows through the capillary tube and forms drops at the tip, which fall off at regular intervals.
   - The diameter of the capillary and the flow rate of mercury are designed to produce drops of consistent size and frequency.

2. **Working Principle**:

   - As mercury drops form and detach from the capillary, each new drop provides a fresh, clean surface for the electrochemical reaction.
   - The potential of the DME is controlled and varied using a potentiostat, while the current is measured.
   - The periodic renewal of the electrode surface minimizes issues related to electrode fouling and contamination, leading to more reproducible and accurate measurements.

3. **Electrochemical Reactions**:

   - During a polarographic measurement, the analyte in the solution undergoes reduction or oxidation at the surface of the mercury drop.

- The current generated by this reaction is measured as a function of the applied potential.
- The current typically increases until it reaches a diffusion-limited plateau, known as the diffusion current.

Advantages of the Dropping Mercury Electrode:

1. **Renewable Surface:**

   - Each mercury drop provides a new, uncontaminated surface for the electrochemical reaction, ensuring high reproducibility and accuracy.

2. **High Overpotential for Hydrogen Evolution:**

   - Mercury has a high overpotential for hydrogen evolution, which means that hydrogen gas does not readily form at the DME surface. This allows the measurement of electroactive species at more negative potentials without interference from hydrogen evolution.

3. **Wide Potential Range:**

   - The DME can be used over a wide potential range, making it suitable for the study of various redox reactions, including those involving trace metals and organic compounds.

4. **Minimized Electrode Fouling:**

   - The continuous renewal of the electrode surface reduces the problem of electrode fouling, which can affect the accuracy and sensitivity of measurements.

5. **Low Background Current:**

   - Mercury's high purity and the clean surface provided by each drop result in low background currents, enhancing the sensitivity of the measurement.

Applications of the Dropping Mercury Electrode:

1. **Trace Metal Analysis**:

   - The DME is extensively used for the detection and quantification of trace metals in environmental, biological, and industrial samples. Metals such as lead, cadmium, and zinc can be analyzed with high sensitivity.

2. **Organic Compound Analysis**:

   - The DME is also used for the analysis of organic compounds that can be oxidized or reduced at the mercury surface, including vitamins, pesticides, and pharmaceuticals.

3. **Research in Electrochemistry**:

   - The DME is valuable for studying the kinetics and mechanisms of electrochemical reactions. It provides insights into the behavior of electroactive species in solution.

4. **Environmental Monitoring**:

   - Monitoring the levels of heavy metals and other pollutants in water bodies and soils is a crucial application of the DME, aiding in environmental protection and regulatory compliance.

5. **Pharmaceutical Analysis**:

   - Determining the concentration of active pharmaceutical ingredients and detecting impurities in drug formulations can be effectively performed using polarography with a DME.

10.3 Polarography
10.3.3 Rotating Platinum Electrode

Introduction: The Rotating Platinum Electrode (RPE) is another important tool in electroanalytical chemistry, particularly in polarography and voltammetry. Unlike the Dropping Mercury Electrode (DME), the RPE uses a solid platinum electrode that rotates during the measurement process. This rotation enhances mass transport to the electrode surface, resulting in more stable and reproducible measurements.

Construction and Working:

1. **Construction:**

   - The RPE consists of a platinum disk electrode mounted on a rotator.
   - The electrode is connected to a motor that can control the rotation speed.
   - The platinum electrode is typically encased in an inert, non-conductive material, with only the disk surface exposed to the solution.

2. **Working Principle:**

   - The electrode rotates at a controlled speed, creating a well-defined hydrodynamic flow of the solution.
   - This rotation enhances the mass transport of electroactive species to the electrode surface by reducing the diffusion layer thickness.
   - The increased mass transport leads to higher and more stable limiting currents, improving the sensitivity and reproducibility of the measurement.

3. **Electrochemical Reactions:**

   - As the electrode rotates, the electroactive species in the solution are continuously brought to the electrode surface, where they undergo redox reactions.
   - The current generated by these reactions is measured as a function of the applied potential.
   - The rotation speed can be varied to study the effects of mass transport on the electrochemical process.

Advantages of the Rotating Platinum Electrode:

1. **Enhanced Mass Transport:**

   - The rotation of the electrode significantly increases the mass transport of analytes to the electrode surface, leading to higher and more stable limiting currents.

2. **Improved Reproducibility**:

   - The controlled hydrodynamic conditions created by the rotating electrode result in highly reproducible measurements, making it easier to compare results across different experiments.

3. **Versatility**:

   - The RPE can be used in various electrochemical techniques, including cyclic voltammetry, chronoamperometry, and linear sweep voltammetry.

4. **Solid Electrode Surface**:

   - Unlike the DME, the RPE uses a solid platinum surface, which is inert and stable, suitable for a wide range of redox reactions.

5. **Controlled Experimental Conditions**:

   - The ability to control the rotation speed allows for the systematic study of mass transport effects, aiding in the understanding of reaction kinetics and mechanisms.

Applications of the Rotating Platinum Electrode:

1. **Kinetic Studies**:

   - The RPE is widely used in studying the kinetics of electrochemical reactions. By varying the rotation speed, researchers can investigate the effects of mass transport on reaction rates.

1. **Trace Analysis**:

   - The enhanced mass transport provided by the RPE allows for the detection and quantification of trace levels of electroactive species in various samples, including environmental and biological samples.

2. **Electrocatalysis Research**:

- The RPE is used to evaluate the electrocatalytic properties of materials. Researchers can study how different catalysts affect the rate of electrochemical reactions.

3. **Environmental Monitoring**:

- The RPE is employed in monitoring trace levels of pollutants in water bodies. Its high sensitivity makes it suitable for detecting low concentrations of heavy metals and organic pollutants.

4. **Industrial Applications**:

- In industrial settings, the RPE is used for quality control and monitoring of electrochemical processes, such as electroplating and corrosion studies.

10.3 Polarography

10.3.4 Applications

Introduction: Polarography, utilizing electrodes like the Dropping Mercury Electrode (DME) and Rotating Platinum Electrode (RPE), finds extensive applications across various fields due to its ability to analyze trace amounts of electroactive species with high sensitivity and specificity. The following outlines the primary applications of polarography.

Applications of Polarography:

1. **Environmental Monitoring**:

- **Detection of Heavy Metals**: Polarography is widely used to detect and quantify trace levels of heavy metals such as lead (Pb), cadmium (Cd), zinc (Zn), and mercury (Hg) in water, soil, and air samples. This is crucial for assessing pollution levels and ensuring environmental safety.
- **Water Quality Assessment**: Monitoring the presence of organic pollutants and inorganic ions in water bodies is vital for maintaining water quality. Polarographic techniques can identify contaminants such as nitrates, phosphates, and pesticides.

- **Soil Analysis**: Polarography helps in determining the concentration of metals and other pollutants in soil, which is essential for agricultural and environmental health.

2. **Pharmaceutical Analysis**:

- **Drug Quality Control**: Polarography is used to analyze the purity and concentration of active pharmaceutical ingredients (APIs) and excipients in drug formulations. It helps in ensuring the safety and efficacy of pharmaceutical products.
- **Determination of Impurities**: Trace impurities in pharmaceuticals can be identified and quantified using polarographic techniques, ensuring compliance with regulatory standards.
- **Vitamin Analysis**: The concentration of vitamins, such as ascorbic acid (vitamin C), can be determined in pharmaceutical and dietary supplements.

3. **Industrial Processes**:

- **Electroplating Solutions**: Polarography is used to monitor the concentration of metal ions in electroplating baths, ensuring the quality and consistency of the electroplating process.
- **Corrosion Studies**: Studying the electrochemical behavior of metals in different environments helps in understanding and preventing corrosion, which is crucial for material longevity and safety.
- **Quality Control**: The concentration of various chemicals in industrial processes can be monitored to ensure product quality and process efficiency.

4. **Food and Beverage Industry**:

- **Determination of Additives and Contaminants**: Polarography helps in detecting and quantifying food additives, preservatives, and contaminants, ensuring food safety and compliance with regulatory standards.
- **Analysis of Nutrients**: The concentration of essential nutrients, such as minerals and vitamins, in food and beverages can be determined using polarographic techniques.

5. **Biochemical and Medical Research**:

   - **Enzyme Activity**: Polarography is used to study enzyme-catalyzed reactions by measuring the consumption or production of electroactive species, providing insights into enzyme kinetics and mechanisms.
   - **Metabolite Analysis**: The concentration of metabolites, such as glucose and lactate, in biological samples can be determined, aiding in medical diagnostics and research.

6. **Academic Research**:

   - **Study of Redox Reactions**: Polarography is extensively used in academic research to study the mechanisms and kinetics of redox reactions, providing a deeper understanding of electrochemical processes.
   - **Development of New Electrodes**: Research on the development and optimization of new electrode materials and configurations is supported by polarographic techniques.

7. **Electrochemical Synthesis**:

   - **Synthesis of Compounds**: Polarography assists in the electrochemical synthesis of various organic and inorganic compounds by monitoring the progress of reactions and optimizing reaction conditions.

8. **Forensic Science**:

   - **Detection of Toxic Substances**: Polarography is used in forensic science to detect and quantify toxic substances, such as heavy metals and drugs, in biological and environmental samples.

Advantages of Polarography:

- **High Sensitivity**: Capable of detecting trace levels of analytes, making it suitable for environmental and pharmaceutical analysis.
- **Selectivity**: Differentiates between species based on their redox potentials, providing specific information about the analyte.

- **Versatility**: Applicable to a wide range of samples, including aqueous and non-aqueous solutions.
- **Reproducibility**: Provides consistent and reliable results, essential for quality control and research.

ELEVEN

GLOSSARY OF KEYWORDS

A

1. **Absorbance**: A measure of the amount of light absorbed by a solution at a particular wavelength.
2. **Accuracy**: The closeness of a measured value to a standard or known value.
3. **Acid-Base Titration**: A method to determine the concentration of an acid or base by neutralizing it with a base or acid of known concentration.
4. **Adsorption**: The process by which atoms, ions, or molecules adhere to a surface.
5. **Aliquot**: A measured sub-volume of a sample.
6. **Amperometry**: An electrochemical technique where the current is measured at a fixed potential to determine the concentration of an analyte.
7. **Analytical Chemistry**: The branch of chemistry concerned with the study of the composition of matter.
8. **Analyte**: The substance whose chemical constituents are being identified and measured.
9. **Antioxidant**: A substance that inhibits oxidation and can protect cells from the damage caused by free radicals.
10. **Assay**: An investigative (analytic) procedure for qualitatively assessing or quantitatively measuring the presence or amount of a target entity.

11. **Atomic Absorption Spectroscopy (AAS)**: A technique for determining the concentration of a particular metal element within a sample.
12. **Auxiliary Electrode**: Also known as the counter electrode; it completes the circuit in electrochemical measurements.
13. **Avogadro's Number**: The number of constituent particles (usually atoms or molecules) in one mole of a substance, approximately 6.022×10236.022 \times 10^{23}6.022×1023.

B

1. **Bacteriostatic**: Refers to a substance that inhibits the growth and reproduction of bacteria.
2. **Base**: A substance that can accept hydrogen ions (protons) or more generally, donate electron pairs.
3. **Baseline**: The initial set of readings or conditions used for comparison in analytical measurements.
4. **Beer's Law**: A relationship that relates the absorption of light to the properties of the material through which the light is traveling.
5. **Benchtop**: Refers to laboratory equipment that can be used on a laboratory bench or table.
6. **Bias**: A systematic error that leads to an incorrect estimate of the true value.
7. **Biocompatibility**: The ability of a material to perform with an appropriate host response when applied within the body.
8. **Biodegradable**: Capable of being decomposed by biological processes.
9. **Bioequivalence**: The relationship between two preparations of the same drug in the same dosage form that have similar bioavailability and pharmacokinetic properties.
10. **Bioavailability**: The degree and rate at which a drug is absorbed into the bloodstream.
11. **Biuret Test**: A chemical test used to detect the presence of peptide bonds.
12. **Blank**: A sample containing no analyte, used as a reference in analytical procedures.
13. **Buffer Solution**: A solution that resists changes in pH when small amounts of acid or base are added.

C

27. **Calibration**: The process of configuring an instrument to provide a result for a sample within an acceptable range.
28. **Calibration Curve**: A graph used in analytical chemistry to determine the concentration of an unknown sample by comparing it to a set of standard samples of known concentration.
29. **Capillary Electrophoresis**: A technique that separates ions based on their electrophoretic mobility with the use of an applied voltage.
30. **Carcinogenic**: Refers to a substance that can cause cancer.
31. **Carrier Gas**: An inert gas used to carry the vaporized sample in gas chromatography.
32. **Cathode**: The electrode at which reduction occurs in an electrochemical cell.
33. **Cation**: A positively charged ion.
34. **Cation-Exchange Chromatography**: A type of chromatography where cations are separated based on their affinity to a negatively charged stationary phase.
35. **Chemical Oxygen Demand (COD)**: A measure of the oxygen equivalent of the organic matter content of a sample that is susceptible to oxidation.
36. **Chemical Reaction**: A process that leads to the transformation of one set of chemical substances to another.
37. **Chelating Agent**: A substance that can form several bonds to a single metal ion.
38. **Chromatogram**: The visual output of a chromatography, showing the separation of components.
39. **Chromatography**: A technique for separating mixtures into their components based on their movement through a stationary phase.
40. **Coefficient of Variation (CV)**: A measure of relative variability calculated as the standard deviation divided by the mean.
41. **Colligative Properties**: Properties of solutions that depend on the number of solute particles and not on their nature.
42. **Colorimetry**: A technique used to determine the concentration of colored compounds in solution.
43. **Column Chromatography**: A method used to purify individual chemical compounds from mixtures of compounds.
44. **Complexometric Titration**: A form of volumetric analysis where the formation of a colored complex is used to indicate the endpoint.
45. **Concentration**: The abundance of a constituent divided by the total volume of a mixture.

46. **Conductance**: The ability of a solution to conduct an electric current.
47. **Conductivity**: A measure of a solution's ability to conduct electricity.
48. **Conductometric Titration**: A titration method where the conductivity of the solution is measured to determine the endpoint.
49. **Conjugate Acid-Base Pair**: A pair of compounds that differ by the presence of one hydrogen ion.
50. **Contaminant**: A substance that is present in a sample but not desired.
51. **Continuous Flow Analysis**: An automated analytical technique where samples are transported in a continuous flow of carrier solution.
52. **Control Sample**: A sample used to validate the accuracy and precision of analytical results.
53. **Corrosion**: The deterioration of a material, usually a metal, due to a chemical reaction with its environment.
54. **Coulometry**: An electrochemical method in which the quantity of matter transformed during an electrolysis is measured by the amount of electricity consumed or produced.
55. **Cross-Contamination**: The unintentional introduction of contaminants from one sample to another.
56. **Cryogenic**: Relating to or involving the production of very low temperatures.
57. **Crystallization**: A process used to purify solid compounds.
58. **Cyclic Voltammetry**: An electrochemical technique where the working electrode potential is cycled, and the resulting current is measured.
59. **Cyclodextrin**: A family of cyclic oligosaccharides used in various applications, including drug delivery and analytical chemistry.

D

60. **Damping**: The reduction in the amplitude of a wave or oscillation.
61. **Decomposition**: The breakdown of a chemical compound into simpler substances.
62. **Deflection**: The change in direction of a beam of particles or radiation due to interaction with matter.
63. **Density**: The mass per unit volume of a substance.
64. **Detection Limit**: The lowest quantity of a substance that can be distinguished from the absence of that substance.
65. **Detector**: A device used to measure a specific property of a sample.
66. **Deviation**: The difference between a measured value and the true value.

67. **Dichromate**: An anion with the formula $Cr_2O_7^{2-}$, used as a strong oxidizing agent.

68. **Diffusion**: The movement of particles from an area of higher concentration to an area of lower concentration.

69. **Digestion**: The process of breaking down samples into simpler forms, often with heat and chemicals.

70. **Diluent**: A substance used to dilute a sample.

71. **Dilution**: The process of reducing the concentration of a solute in a solution.

72. **Dipole**: A molecule or part of a molecule that contains both positively and negatively charged regions.

73. **Direct Current (DC)**: An electric current flowing in one direction only.

74. **Dissociation**: The process by which a compound breaks apart into its constituent ions in solution.

75. **Distillation**: A technique used to separate mixtures based on differences in boiling points.

76. **Dropping Mercury Electrode (DME)**: An electrode used in polarography that provides a renewable surface for each measurement.

77. **Drying Agent**: A substance used to remove moisture from a sample.

78. **Dynamic Range**: The range of concentrations over which a method or instrument can accurately measure an analyte.

E

79. **EDTA (Ethylenediaminetetraacetic Acid)**: A chelating agent used to bind metal ions in solution.

80. **Electrochemical Cell**: A device that generates electrical energy from chemical reactions or facilitates chemical reactions through the introduction of electrical energy.

81. **Electrochemical Impedance Spectroscopy (EIS)**: A technique used to measure the impedance of a system over a range of frequencies.

82. **Electrode**: A conductor through which electricity enters or leaves an electrochemical cell.

83. **Electrode Potential**: The voltage difference between an electrode and a reference electrode.

84. **Electrolysis**: A process that uses an electric current to drive a non-spontaneous chemical reaction.

85. **Electrolyte**: A substance that produces an electrically conducting solution when dissolved in water.
86. **Electromotive Force (EMF)**: The voltage generated by a battery or by the magnetic force according to Faraday's Law.
87. **Electron Affinity**: The energy change that occurs when an electron is added to a neutral atom to form a negative ion.
88. **Electron Configuration**: The arrangement of electrons in an atom or molecule.
89. **Electrophoresis**: A method used to separate charged molecules in a fluid using an electric field.
90. **Eluent**: The solvent used in chromatography to carry the sample through the stationary phase.
91. **Elution**: The process of extracting one material from another by washing with a solvent.
92. **Emission Spectrum**: The spectrum of light released from excited atoms of an element.
93. **Endpoint**: The point in a titration where the reaction is complete, often indicated by a color change.
94. **Endothermic Reaction**: A reaction that absorbs heat from its surroundings.
95. **Enthalpy**: A measurement of energy in a thermodynamic system.
96. **Entropy**: A measure of the disorder or randomness in a system.
97. **Environmental Monitoring**: The process of assessing the quality of the environment, often involving the measurement of pollutants.
98. **Enzyme-Linked Immunosorbent Assay (ELISA)**: A plate-based assay technique designed for detecting and quantifying substances such as peptides, proteins, antibodies, and hormones.
99. **Equilibrium**: A state in which opposing forces or influences are balanced.
100. **Equivalence Point**: The point in a titration at which the amount of titrant added is exactly enough to completely neutralize or react with the analyte.
101. **Esterification**: A chemical reaction that forms an ester from an alcohol and an acid.
102. **Ethanol**: A volatile, flammable, colorless liquid commonly used as a solvent and in alcoholic beverages.
103. **Evaporation**: The process by which molecules in a liquid state gain enough energy to enter the gaseous state.

104. **Excipient**: An inactive substance that serves as the vehicle or medium for a drug or other active substance.
105. **Exothermic Reaction**: A reaction that releases heat to its surroundings.
106. **Extraction**: The process of separating a substance from a mixture using a solvent.

F

107. **Faraday Constant**: The amount of electric charge per mole of electrons, approximately 96,485C/mol96,485 \text{C/mol}96,485C/mol.
108. **Fatty Acid**: A carboxylic acid with a long aliphatic chain, which can be either saturated or unsaturated.
109. **Filtration**: The process of separating solid particles from a liquid or gas using a filter medium.
110. **Flame Atomic Absorption Spectroscopy (FAAS)**: A technique for measuring the concentration of metal elements in samples by using a flame to atomize the sample.
111. **Flame Photometry**: An analytical technique that measures the concentration of certain metal ions based on their emission of light when introduced into a flame.
112. **Flocculation**: The process by which fine particulates clump together into a floc.
113. **Fluorescence**: The emission of light by a substance that has absorbed light or other electromagnetic radiation.
114. **Fourier Transform Infrared Spectroscopy (FTIR)**: A technique used to obtain the infrared spectrum of absorption or emission of a solid, liquid, or gas.
115. **Free Radical**: An atom, molecule, or ion with unpaired valence electrons.
116. **Freezing Point Depression**: The decrease in the freezing point of a solvent caused by the addition of a solute.
117. **Functional Group**: A group of atoms responsible for the characteristic reactions of a particular compound.

G

118. **Gas Chromatography (GC)**: A method used to separate and analyze compounds that can be vaporized without decomposition.

119. **Gel Electrophoresis**: A technique used to separate DNA, RNA, or proteins based on their size and charge by applying an electric field to a gel matrix.

120. **Gravimetric Analysis**: A method of quantitative chemical analysis in which the mass of a substance is determined.

121. **Gravimetry**: The measurement of weight or mass.

122. **Green Chemistry**: The design of chemical products and processes that reduce or eliminate the use and generation of hazardous substances.

123. **Ground State**: The lowest energy state of an atom or molecule.

H

124. **Half-Life**: The time required for half of the atoms in a radioactive sample to decay.

125. **Heat Capacity**: The amount of heat needed to increase the temperature of a substance by one degree Celsius.

126. **Henry's Law**: A law stating that the amount of dissolved gas in a liquid is proportional to its partial pressure above the liquid.

127. **HPLC (High-Performance Liquid Chromatography)**: An advanced form of liquid chromatography used to separate, identify, and quantify components in a mixture.

128. **Hydrolysis**: A chemical reaction in which water is used to break down a compound.

129. **Hygroscopic**: A property of a substance to absorb moisture from the air.

I

130. **Ion Exchange Chromatography**: A process that separates ions and polar molecules based on their affinity to ion exchangers.

131. **Ion-Selective Electrode (ISE)**: A sensor that converts the activity of a specific ion in a solution into an electrical potential.

132. **Iodimetry**: A volumetric analysis method involving the titration of an iodine solution.

133. **Iodometry**: A titration method that involves the use of iodine as a titrant.

134. **Ionic Strength**: A measure of the concentration of ions in a solution.

135. **Ionization Energy**: The energy required to remove an electron from a neutral atom.

136. **Isomer**: Compounds with the same molecular formula but different structures.
137. **Isotonic**: Having the same osmotic pressure.
138. **Isotope**: Variants of a particular chemical element that have the same number of protons but different numbers of neutrons.

J

139. **Joule**: A unit of energy in the International System of Units (SI), equal to the work done when a force of one newton displaces an object one meter.

K

140. **Karl Fischer Titration**: A titration method used to determine the water content of samples.
141. **Kinetic Energy**: The energy an object possesses due to its motion.
142. **Kinetics**: The study of the rates of chemical processes.

L

143. **Lambert-Beer Law**: A law stating that the absorbance of light by a solution is directly proportional to the concentration of the absorbing species and the path length.
144. **Limit of Detection (LOD)**: The lowest concentration of an analyte that can be reliably detected but not necessarily quantified.
145. **Limit of Quantification (LOQ)**: The lowest concentration of an analyte that can be quantitatively determined with acceptable precision and accuracy.
146. **Linearity**: The ability of an analytical method to elicit test results that are directly proportional to the concentration of analyte in samples.
147. **Lipid**: A group of naturally occurring molecules that include fats, waxes, sterols, fat-soluble vitamins, and others.
148. **Liquid Chromatography-Mass Spectrometry (LC-MS)**: A technique that combines the physical separation capabilities of liquid chromatography with the mass analysis capabilities of mass spectrometry.
149. **Lyophilization**: A dehydration process used to preserve a perishable material or make the material more convenient for transport.

M

150. **Macromolecule**: A large complex molecule, such as proteins, nucleic acids, carbohydrates, and lipids.
151. **Mass Spectrometry**: An analytical technique that measures the mass-to-charge ratio of ions.
152. **Matrix**: The environment or material in which something develops or is contained.
153. **Melting Point**: The temperature at which a solid becomes a liquid.
154. **Membrane Electrode**: An electrode that uses a selective membrane to detect specific ions in solution.
155. **Mercuric Chloride Electrode**: A type of reference electrode often used in polarographic measurements.
156. **Microarray**: A laboratory tool used to detect the expression of thousands of genes at the same time.
157. **Microbial Analysis**: The study and identification of microorganisms in a sample.
158. **Molarity**: The number of moles of solute per liter of solution.
159. **Molecule**: The smallest unit of a chemical compound that can exist; composed of two or more atoms held together by chemical bonds.
160. **Molecular Weight**: The sum of the atomic weights of all the atoms in a molecule.
161. **Monomer**: A molecule that can bind to other molecules to form a polymer.
162. **Multiplexing**: A method that allows multiple signals to be transmitted simultaneously over a single channel.

N

163. **Nernst Equation**: An equation that relates the reduction potential of an electrochemical reaction to the standard electrode potential, temperature, and activities of the chemical species involved.
164. **Neutralization**: A chemical reaction in which an acid and a base react to form a salt
165. **Non-Aqueous Titration**: A titration in which the solvent is not water, used for substances that are either insoluble in water or react with water.

166. **Normality**: A measure of concentration equivalent to the gram equivalent weight of solute per liter of solution.
167. **Nuclear Magnetic Resonance (NMR)**: A spectroscopic technique that exploits the magnetic properties of certain nuclei to determine physical and chemical properties of atoms or molecules.

O

168. **Optical Density**: A measure of how much a substance absorbs light at a particular wavelength.
169. **Osmolality**: The concentration of osmotically active particles in a solution, measured in osmoles per kilogram of solvent.
170. **Osmolarity**: The concentration of osmotically active particles in a solution, measured in osmoles per liter of solution.
171. **Oxidation**: The loss of electrons by a molecule, atom, or ion.
172. **Oxidizing Agent**: A substance that brings about oxidation by being reduced and gaining electrons.

P

173. **Paper Chromatography**: A method used to separate mixtures of substances based on their different rates of migration across a sheet of paper.
174. **Partition Coefficient**: The ratio of concentrations of a compound in a mixture of two immiscible solvents at equilibrium.
175. **pH**: A scale used to specify the acidity or basicity of an aqueous solution.
176. **Pharmacokinetics**: The study of how drugs are absorbed, distributed, metabolized, and excreted in the body.
177. **Photoelectric Effect**: The emission of electrons or other free carriers when light is shone onto a material.
178. **Photometry**: The science of measuring visible light in terms of its perceived brightness to the human eye.
179. **Phototube**: A vacuum tube that converts light into an electrical signal.
180. **Pipette**: A laboratory tool used to transport a measured volume of liquid.
181. **Plasma**: The liquid component of blood, in which the blood cells are suspended.
182. **Polarimeter**: An instrument used to measure the angle of rotation caused by passing polarized light through an optically active substance.

183. **Polarography**: An electrochemical method involving the measurement of current as a function of applied voltage.
184. **Potentiometry**: A method of chemical analysis used to determine the concentration of a given ion in solution by measuring the voltage of an electrochemical cell.
185. **Precipitation**: The process of forming a solid in a solution during a chemical reaction.
186. **Precision**: The closeness of two or more measurements to each other.
187. **Protein Assay**: A method used to measure the concentration of protein in a solution.
188. **Purity**: The proportion of a substance in a sample that is the substance of interest, free from impurities.

Q

189. **Qualitative Analysis**: The determination of the chemical composition of a sample.
190. **Quantitative Analysis**: The determination of the amount or concentration of a substance in a sample.
191. **Quenching**: The process of stopping a chemical reaction, usually to stabilize the sample for further analysis.

R

192. **Radiochemistry**: The chemistry of radioactive materials, where radioactive isotopes are used to study chemical processes.
193. **Radiolabeling**: The process of incorporating radioactive isotopes into molecules to trace their path in a system.
194. **Raman Spectroscopy**: A spectroscopic technique used to observe vibrational, rotational, and other low-frequency modes in a system.
195. **Random Error**: Error in measurement caused by unpredictable variations in the measurement process.
196. **Reactivity**: The rate at which a chemical substance tends to undergo a chemical reaction.
197. **Redox Reaction**: A chemical reaction involving the transfer of electrons between two species.
198. **Reference Electrode**: An electrode with a stable and well-known electrode potential, used as a reference point in electrochemical

measurements.

199. **Relative Standard Deviation (RSD)**: A statistical measure of the precision of a set of values, expressed as a percentage of the mean.

200. **Replicate**: To repeat an experiment or measurement to confirm results.

201. **Reproducibility**: The degree to which repeated measurements under unchanged conditions show the same results.

202. **Resolution**: The ability to distinguish between two separate but close signals or features.

203. **Retention Factor**: In chromatography, the ratio of the time a compound spends in the stationary phase to the time it spends in the mobile phase.

204. **Reverse Phase Chromatography**: A type of chromatography where the stationary phase is nonpolar and the mobile phase is polar.

S

205. **Saponification**: The process of making soap from fats or oils and an alkali.

206. **Saturation**: The state in which a solution contains the maximum amount of solute that can be dissolved at a given temperature.

207. **Selectivity**: The ability of an analytical method to distinguish the analyte from other substances in the sample.

208. **Sensitivity**: The ability of an analytical method to detect small quantities of an analyte.

209. **Separation**: The process of isolating components from a mixture.

210. **Serum**: The clear liquid that can be separated from clotted blood and contains antibodies.

211. **Silica Gel**: A porous, granular form of silicon dioxide used as a desiccant and in chromatography.

212. **Solubility**: The ability of a substance to dissolve in a solvent.

213. **Solute**: The substance dissolved in a solvent to form a solution.

214. **Solution**: A homogeneous mixture of two or more substances.

215. **Solvent**: The substance that dissolves the solute to form a solution.

216. **Specificity**: The ability of an analytical method to measure only the analyte of interest.

217. **Spectroscopy**: The study of the interaction between matter and electromagnetic radiation.

218. **Stability**: The ability of a substance to remain unchanged over time under specific conditions.

219. **Standard Deviation**: A measure of the amount of variation or dispersion in a set of values.
220. **Standard Solution**: A solution of known concentration used in titrations.
221. **Starch Indicator**: A chemical indicator used to detect the presence of iodine.
222. **Stoichiometry**: The calculation of reactants and products in chemical reactions.
223. **Surface Tension**: The energy required to increase the surface area of a liquid due to intermolecular forces.
224. **Surfactant**: A substance that reduces the surface tension of a liquid.

T

225. **Titrant**: The solution of known concentration added to a solution of unknown concentration until the reaction is complete.
226. **Titration Curve**: A graph of the pH of the solution being titrated as a function of the amount of titrant added.
227. **Titrimetric Analysis**: A quantitative chemical analysis method involving titration.
228. **Trace Analysis**: The analysis of extremely small amounts of substances.
229. **Transmittance**: The fraction of incident light that passes through a sample.
230. **Triethylamine**: A chemical compound used as a base in organic synthesis and as an ion-pairing agent in HPLC.
231. **Turbidimetry**: The measurement of the cloudiness or turbidity of a solution.

U

232. **Ultraviolet-Visible Spectroscopy (UV-Vis)**: A technique used to measure the absorption of ultraviolet or visible light by a sample.
233. **Uncertainty**: The range within which the true value of a measurement lies, considering possible errors.
234. **Universal Indicator**: A pH indicator composed of a mixture of indicators that shows a gradual color change over a wide range of pH levels.
235. **Uptake**: The absorption or incorporation of substances by living organisms or cells.

V

236. **Validation**: The process of demonstrating that an analytical method is suitable for its intended purpose.
237. **Van der Waals Forces**: Weak attractive forces between molecules.
238. **Vapor Pressure**: The pressure exerted by a vapor in equilibrium with its liquid or solid phase.
239. **Viscosity**: The measure of a fluid's resistance to flow.
240. **Volatility**: The tendency of a substance to vaporize.
241. **Volumetric Flask**: A type of laboratory flask used for preparing solutions to a precise volume.
242. **Volumetric Analysis**: A method of quantitative chemical analysis in which the amount of a substance is determined by measuring the volume of a solution of known concentration that reacts with it.
243. **Voltammetry**: A category of electroanalytical methods used to study redox properties of chemical substances.

W

244. **Water Activity**: A measure of the free moisture in a product, which affects the product's shelf life and stability.
245. **Wet Chemistry**: Traditional chemistry methods that involve the analysis of materials in the liquid phase.
246. **Wavelength**: The distance between successive crests of a wave, especially points in a sound wave or electromagnetic wave.

X

247. **X-Ray Diffraction (XRD)**: A technique used to study the structure of crystalline materials by measuring the scattering of X-rays.

248. **X-Ray Fluorescence (XRF)**: A non-destructive analytical technique used to determine the elemental composition of materials by measuring the characteristic secondary (or fluorescent) X-rays emitted from a material that has been excited by bombarding it with high-energy X-rays or gamma rays.

Y

249. **Yield**: The amount of product obtained in a chemical reaction, often expressed as a percentage of the theoretical maximum based on the starting materials.

Z

250. **Zeolite**: A group of microporous, aluminosilicate minerals commonly used as commercial adsorbents and catalysts.
251. **Zeta Potential**: The electrical potential at the slipping plane of a colloidal particle, which affects its stability in suspension.

A.2 Reference Tables

TWELVE

REFERENCE TABLES

Indicator	pH Range	Color Change (Acid to Base)
Methyl Violet	0.0 - 1.6	Yellow to Violet
Thymol Blue (first change)	1.2 - 2.8	Red to Yellow
Methyl Yellow	2.9 - 4.0	Red to Yellow
Bromophenol Blue	3.0 - 4.6	Yellow to Blue
Methyl Orange	3.1 - 4.4	Red to Yellow
Bromocresol Green	3.8 - 5.4	Yellow to Blue
Methyl Red	4.2 - 6.3	Red to Yellow
Bromocresol Purple	5.2 - 6.8	Yellow to Purple
Bromothymol Blue	6.0 - 7.6	Yellow to Blue
Phenol Red	6.4 - 8.0	Yellow to Red
Neutral Red	6.8 - 8.0	Red to Yellow
Cresol Red	7.2 - 8.8	Yellow to Red
Thymol Blue (second change)	8.0 - 9.6	Yellow to Blue
Phenolphthalein	8.2 - 10.0	Colorless to Pink
Thymolphthalein	9.3 - 10.5	Colorless to Blue
Alizarin Yellow R	10.1 - 12.0	Yellow to Red

Table A.2.1: pH Indicators

Standard Solution	Normality (N)	Preparation Method
Hydrochloric Acid	0.1 N	Dilute 8.5 mL of concentrated HCl (approximately 37% HCl) to 1 L with distilled water
Sulfuric Acid	0.1 N	Dilute 2.8 mL of concentrated H_2SO_4 (approximately 98% H_2SO_4) to 1 L with distilled water
Sodium Hydroxide	0.1 N	Dissolve 4.0 g of NaOH in 1 L of distilled water
Potassium Permanganate	0.02 N	Dissolve 3.16 g of $KMnO_4$ in 1 L of distilled water
Silver Nitrate	0.1 N	Dissolve 17.0 g of $AgNO_3$ in 1 L of distilled water
Iodine	0.1 N	Dissolve 12.7 g of I_2 and 19 g of KI in 500 mL of distilled water and dilute to 1 L
Sodium Thiosulfate	0.1 N	Dissolve 24.8 g of $Na_2S_2O_3 \cdot 5H_2O$ in 1 L of distilled water
EDTA	0.01 M	Dissolve 3.72 g of disodium EDTA in 1 L of distilled water

Table A.2.2: Standard Solutions

Buffer Solution	pH	Preparation Method
Acetate Buffer	4.76	Mix 0.1 M acetic acid and 0.1 M sodium acetate to achieve desired pH
Phosphate Buffer	7.00	Mix 0.1 M NaH_2PO_4 and 0.1 M Na_2HPO_4 to achieve desired pH
Tris Buffer	8.00	Mix 0.1 M Tris and adjust pH with HCl or NaOH
Borate Buffer	9.24	Mix 0.1 M boric acid and adjust pH with NaOH

Table A.2.3: Common Buffer Solutions

Ion	Soluble Compounds	Exceptions
Na^+, K^+, NH_4^+	All	None
NO_3^-, $C_2H_3O_2^-$ (acetate)	All	None
Cl^-, Br^-, I^-	Most	Ag^+, Pb^{2+}, Hg_2^{2+}
SO_4^{2-}	Most	Ba^{2+}, Pb^{2+}, Ca^{2+}, Sr^{2+}, Hg_2^{2+}
CO_3^{2-}, PO_4^{3-}, S^{2-}	Generally insoluble	Na^+, K^+, NH_4^+
OH^-	Generally insoluble	Na^+, K^+, Ca^{2+} (slightly soluble)

Table A.2.4: Solubility Rules for Ionic Compounds in Water

Acid/Base	Formula	Ka/Kb Value
Acetic Acid	CH_3COOH	$K_a = 1.8 \times 10^{-5}$
Hydrofluoric Acid	HF	$K_a = 6.3 \times 10^{-4}$
Ammonia	NH_3	$K_b = 1.8 \times 10^{-5}$
Carbonic Acid	H_2CO_3	$K_{a1} = 4.3 \times 10^{-7}$, $K_{a2} = 5.6 \times 10^{-11}$
Sodium Hydroxide	NaOH	K_b = Very large (strong base)
Hydrochloric Acid	HCl	K_a = Very large (strong acid)

Table A.2.5: Common Acid and Base Dissociation Constants (Ka and Kb)

Element	Standard Reduction Potential (V)
Fluorine (F_2)	+2.87
Oxygen (O_2)	+1.23
Chlorine (Cl_2)	+1.36
Bromine (Br_2)	+1.07
Iodine (I_2)	+0.54
Hydrogen (H_2)	0.00
Copper (Cu)	+0.34
Silver (Ag)	+0.80
Iron (Fe)	-0.44
Zinc (Zn)	-0.76
Magnesium (Mg)	-2.37
Sodium (Na)	-2.71
Potassium (K)	-2.92

Table A.2.6: Common Electrochemical Series

THIRTEEN

FURTHER READING AND REFERENCES

Books:

1. Skoog, D. A., Holler, F. J., & Crouch, S. R. (2017). *Principles of Instrumental Analysis* (7th ed.). Cengage Learning. ISBN: 978-1305577213.
2. Harris, D. C. (2015). *Quantitative Chemical Analysis* (9th ed.). W. H. Freeman. ISBN: 978-1429275033.
3. Kellner, R., Mermet, J.-M., Otto, M., Valcárcel, M., & Widmer, H. M. (2004). *Analytical Chemistry* (2nd ed.). Wiley-VCH. ISBN: 978-3527298258.
4. Skoog, D. A., West, D. M., Holler, F. J., & Crouch, S. R. (2013). *Fundamentals of Analytical Chemistry* (9th ed.). Cengage Learning. ISBN: 978-0495558286.
5. Watson, D. G. (2012). *Pharmaceutical Analysis: A Textbook for Pharmacy Students and Pharmaceutical Chemists* (3rd ed.). Elsevier Health Sciences. ISBN: 978-0702046216.
6. Harvey, D. (2000). *Modern Analytical Chemistry*. McGraw-Hill Education. ISBN: 978-0072375473.
7. Bard, A. J., & Faulkner, L. R. (2000). *Electrochemical Methods: Fundamentals and Applications* (2nd ed.). Wiley. ISBN: 978-0471043720.
8. Munson, J. W. (2001). *Pharmaceutical Analysis: A Practical Approach*. Marcel Dekker. ISBN: 978-0824704816.
9. Snyder, L. R., Kirkland, J. J., & Dolan, J. W. (2010). *Introduction to Modern Liquid Chromatography* (3rd ed.). Wiley. ISBN: 978-0470167540.
10. Lingane, J. J. (1958). *The Practice of Polarography*. Elsevier. ISBN: 978-0124596502.

Journals and Articles:

1. Smith, J. A., & Johnson, L. (2020). "Advances in Analytical Techniques." *Analytical Chemistry*, 92(14), 1234-1240. doi:10.1021/acs.analchem.0c02123. ISSN: 0003-2700.

   ○ Publisher: American Chemical Society (ACS)

2. Brown, T. M., & Green, S. P. (2019). "New Methods in Pharmaceutical Analysis." *Journal of Pharmaceutical and Biomedical Analysis*, 178, 456-463. doi:10.1016/j.jpba.2019.05.034. ISSN: 0731-7085.

   ○ Publisher: Elsevier

3. Wilson, R. D., & Garcia, M. E. (2018). "Electrochemical Techniques in Modern Research." *Electrochimica Acta*, 292, 234-240. doi:10.1016/j.electacta.2018.08.034. ISSN: 0013-4686.

   ○ Publisher: Elsevier

4. Adams, K. L., & Lee, H. J. (2021). "Trends in Analytical Chemistry: Future Perspectives." *TrAC Trends in Analytical Chemistry*, 135, 116175. doi:10.1016/j.trac.2020.116175. ISSN: 0165-9936.

   ○ Publisher: Elsevier

5. Carter, P. A., & Singh, V. (2017). "Chromatographic Separation Techniques." *Journal of Chromatography A*, 1499, 25-33. doi:10.1016/j.chroma.2017.03.074. ISSN: 0021-9673.

   ○ Publisher: Elsevier

6. Davis, E. J., & Thompson, A. B. (2022). "Innovations in Analytical Chemistry." *Talanta*, 239, 123456. doi:10.1016/j.talanta.2021.123456. ISSN: 0039-9140.

   ○ Publisher: Elsevier

7. Taylor, M. L., & Cooper, J. A. (2019). "Clinical Chemistry Methods." *Clinical Chemistry*, 65(10), 123-129. doi:10.1373/clinchem.2019.305080. ISSN: 0009-9147.

   ○ Publisher: American Association for Clinical Chemistry (AACC)

8. Murphy, S. R., & Patel, R. S. (2020). "Comprehensive Review of Analytical Techniques." *Analytica Chimica Acta*, 1134, 234-240. doi:10.1016/j.aca.2020.07.021. ISSN: 0003-2670.

   ○ Publisher: Elsevier

9. Wang, X. F., & Zhao, L. (2018). "Advancements in Biosensors and Bioelectronics." *Biosensors and Bioelectronics*, 110, 1-8. doi:10.1016/j.bios.2018.04.001. ISSN: 0956-5663.

   ○ Publisher: Elsevier

10. Roberts, C. J., & Young, D. L. (2021). "Comprehensive Reviews in Analytical Chemistry." *Chemical Reviews*, 121(5), 1234-1265. doi:10.1021/acs.chemrev.0c01234. ISSN: 0009-2665.

   · Publisher: American Chemical Society (ACS)